Hard, Metal & Nu

How to Play

Rock

Michael Heatley, Alan Brown
& Leon Gruszecki

**FLAME TREE
PUBLISHING**

Publisher and Creative Director: Nick Wells
Project Editor: Sara Robson
Music Composition: Leon Gruszecki
Guitars and Consultant: Jake Jackson
New Photography: Stephen Feather
Art Director: Mike Spender
Layout Design: Jake

Special thanks to: Cat Emslie, Chris Herbert and Petra Jones

08 10 12 11 09
1 3 5 7 9 10 8 6 4 2

This edition first published 2008 by
FLAME TREE PUBLISHING
Crabtree Hall, Crabtree Lane
Fulham, London SW6 6TY
United Kingdom

www.flametreepublishing.com

Flame Tree Publishing is part of the Foundry Creative Media Co. Ltd

© 2008 this edition The Foundry Creative Media Co. Ltd

ISBN 978-1-84786-199-3

A CIP record for this book is available from the British
Library upon request.

Acknowledgements
All photographs and notation courtesy of Foundry Arts, except the following:
courtesy of Corbis 9 © Rune Hellestad, 10 © Mitchell Gerber, 13 © Joe Giron,
15 & 18 & 373 © Neal Preston, 19 Paul Reed Smith Guitars, 26 © John Atashian,
369 courtesy of Gibson Guitars, 381 © Contographer®; courtesy of
Shutterstock 57, 83, 109, 135, 161, 187, 213, 239, 265, 291, 317, 343; courtesy
of Redferns/David Redfern 370.

Michael Heatley (Text) has written over 100 books, has penned liner notes
to more than 100 CD reissues, and written for magazines including *Music
Week*, *Billboard*, *Goldmine*, *Radio Times* and *Record Collector*. More recently he
was the author of *How to Write Great Songs* also published by Flame Tree.

Alan Brown (Musical Examples). A former member of the Scottish National
Orchestra, Alan now works as a freelance musician, with several leading UK
orchestras, and as a consultant in music and IT. Alan has had several compositions
published, developed a set of music theory CD-Roms, co-written a series of Bass
Guitar Examination Handbooks and worked on over 100 further titles.

Printed in China

Contents

Key Terms

ALTERNATE PICKING Using upward and downward strokes alternately when using a pick (*see* page 42).

ARPEGGIO A broken chord in which the notes are played in succession rather than simultaneously.

DISTORTION Distorted, harsh or fuzzy sound created either accidentally or deliberately through overdriven amplification or distortion pedals (*see* pages 46 & 51).

FEEDBACK The 'ringing' or 'howling' sound produced when pickups or microphones pick up the sound they produce through loudspeakers and feed it back creating a sound loop (*see* page 51).

HAMMER-ON A technique involving 'hammering' a finger onto a higher point on a string after that string has just been played, in order to achieve smoother playing, or 'slurs' (*see* pages 34 & 37–38). *See also* 'Pull-off'.

HUMBUCKER A two-coil guitar pickup designed to 'buck the hum' (*see* page 19).

LEGATO Playing notes in smooth succession, with no silent intervals, usually with 'hammer-ons' and 'pull-offs' (*see* page 44).

LICK A distinct guitar phrase (*see* page 16).

OPEN TUNING Where the guitar is tuned so that a chord can be played without fretting any of the strings (using the left hand to press down the strings; *see* page 30).

OVERDRIVE A form of usually deliberate guitar distortion produced by running the amplifiers at overly high volume so that a 'growl' or 'edge' can be heard (*see* pages 22, 41 & 53).

PALM MUTING Using the side or heel of the right hand to dampen the strings close to the bridge while playing (*see* page 45).

PICKUP A device, usually mounted on the body of the guitar underneath the strings, which picks up the mechanical vibrations and turns them into an electrical signal which can be amplified (*see* pages 19–20, 49 & 51).

PINCH HARMONIC Using the thumb to dampen the 'fundamental' sound after picking a note in order to leave the 'harmonic' (*see* page 47).

PLECTRUM A small, plastic tool, usually triangular, which is used to pick the guitar strings (and sometimes called a 'pick'; *see* page 35).

POWER CHORD A chord composed of the root and fifth notes but missing its major or minor third and played with distortion in order to sound more powerful (*see* page 40).

PULL-OFF A technique involving 'pulling' a finger off a string to leave another finger still on the string lower down, after that string has just been played, in order to achieve smoother playing, or 'slurs' (*see* pages 34, 37 & 42–44). *See also* 'Hammer-on'.

RIFF A repeated guitar phrase that forms the 'hook' of the song (*see* page 16).

SHREDDING/SHRED GUITAR An all-encompassing term describing the playing of rapid musical passages on electric guitar using sweep-picking, hammer-ons, pull-offs and other techniques (*see* page 15 & 42).

SWEEP-PICKING Mainly used for arpeggios, this technique involves using a sweeping motion of the pick hand and matching the motion in the fretting hand, in order to achieve a fast and smooth series of notes (*see* page 42).

TAPPING Using the fingers of one hand to 'tap' the strings against the fingerboard (while fretting the strings with the other hand) to produce legato notes (*see* page 44).

TREMOLO ARM A lever that is pulled and pushed to achieve a vibrato effect by changing the pitch of the strings (*see* page 20).

WHAMMY BAR *See* 'Tremolo arm'.

Introduction

Ever since the electric guitar as we know it was created, the urge to plug in and rock out has been one of the most primal known to young men. And even today, in this computerized age where anyone with a PC thinks they're a musician, this remains the case. The lure of six strings, an amplifier and the ability to make a raucous noise has weathered every fad or fashion.

It was at the end of the Sixties that the courses of pop and rock diverged. Rock chose to put record sales a distant second to musical credibility, and bands working from a blues base came to create something more rewarding for its players and listeners than the radio-friendly three-minute singles of old. The vinyl album, with 20 minutes a side, offered more possibilities to explore – and the likes of Led Zeppelin did just that. As venues changed from clubs to stadia, the volume grew too, and heavy metal was born.

The term 'heavy metal' is generally thought to have originated in 'Born To Be Wild', the biker anthem recorded by Steppenwolf in the late Sixties. The lyric refers to 'heavy metal thunder', and that was certainly an apt description of the music that dominated the early Seventies. There have been peaks and troughs of popularity since, but not only has it survived, it has thrived as one of the most durable musical forms.

The dividing line between heavy metal and hard rock is blurred, as are those between the other genres. This is because rock is constantly evolving, one style having its roots in another. You may have seen these labels dividing the racks in your local music megastore, but bands themselves will rarely define themselves. In other words, use these terms if they help; smile and turn a blind eye if they do not.

As for 'nu rock' or 'nu metal', the terms explain themselves – while metal drifted out of fashion in the Nineties it never went away completely. Bands like Korn, Limp Bizkit, Slipknot, Deftones, Amen and Papa Roach revived it and brought it back with a bang as the decade ended. There have also been crossovers with other kinds of music, notably rap and hip-hop – though this was nothing new, Aerosmith and Run-DMC being the first to do this back in 1986. But the guitar has continued to be the driving force, and always will be.

Most important, however, is to change how you define yourself – from listener to participant. So pick up your guitar and begin your own personal voyage of exploration.

The Elements

The Sounds

The ingredients of the various rock genres are relatively constant: guitars, bass, drums, vocals and occasionally keyboards. What varies is the styles applied and the quantities in which they are used. When you realize that the main point that differentiates death metal from black metal is that singers in death metal bands favour a lower, more guttural delivery than the screamed vocals of black metal, it is clear that there will be much overlap between genres. After all, what's a sore throat between friends?

Lyrically, heavy metal has addressed angst and frustration rather than the plastic 'moon in June' scenarios of the pop world, but there has also been a fair sprinkling of sword and sorcery stirred into the mix. As other genres of rock have been created, they have claimed their own lyrical preoccupations: death, doom and black metal unsurprisingly favour pessimistic subjects. Hard rock is less restricted, allowing such anthems as Guns N'Roses' 'Sweet Child O'Mine', while goth has spanned a wide constituency from the chart-worthy Cure to American post-punks Christian Death. Goth rock,

moreover, promotes the bass as a lead instrument to rank almost alongside the guitar, which makes it both unusual and distinctive.

Musically, the styles covered in this book range from the deliberately challenging sound of grindcore, described by DJ John Peel as 'beyond any aggressive music heard before' to the rock-rap and rock-funk hybrids of nu metal and alternative metal. And while grindcore might struggle for airplay now the late lamented Peel has departed, Limp Bizkit and the Chili Peppers, nu and alternative metal heroes respectively, have had no such problems in their heyday. Yet radio play depends on current popularity, and the genres of rock we are examining here depend more on grassroots support than today's fashions.

Some rock genres, like thrash and speed metal, depend on high tempo, high energy playing that

stemmed from the early-Eighties new wave. Doom metal is both tuned down and slowed down, while goth can vary between the extremes. Virtuoso metal never disappears, as there is a whole subculture dedicated to appreciating guitarists of the calibre of Eddie Van Halen and Yngwie Malmsteen, and learning to 'shred' is a rite of passage for any self-respecting teenage guitar player.

The Line Ups

When it comes to rock music, the six-string guitar is always the defining musical element. That is not to say the bass, drums and vocal do not have important parts to play, but it is inevitably the riff on which the success or failure of the venture rides.

Playing rock or metal guitar is all about riffs and licks. So what's the difference? A riff is a lick or phrase that is repeated so often that it forms the 'hook' to a song, while a lick may crop up only once or twice but is a recognizable component of a solo or lead part. So a lick can be a riff, but a riff is usually something more substantial altogether.

The bass and drums, collectively known as the rhythm section, lock together to power the band. In numbers employing a typical 'four-four' time signature, the bass guitar will sync into the bass drum pattern to play anything from four to sixteen notes per 'bar' of music. The speed and intensity of this bass pattern will do much to shape the feel of the song. So too will the tempo of the drumming, as this is the foundation on which the music is built. The advent of the double bass drum in the late Seventies played a major part in propelling thrash and speed metal to even greater velocity.

Keyboards are a relatively rare commodity in rock, but a competent player can be more than worth their place – especially in hard rock, where a Hammond organ is often a component of a blues-based sound, or prog metal where bands like Dream Theater build up impressive layers of sound with synthesizers.

Vocals and vocalists in rock are a law unto themselves. The singer is often initially nominated by virtue of being the least proficient instrumentalist, but he or she stands alongside the guitarist as the most recognizable face of the band. And it is arguable that more successful bands have survived a change of guitarist than singer (Van Halen and Iron Maiden perhaps the obvious exceptions).

But great frontmen will be pulled down by an incompetent rhythm section, and the best bass and drummer will stand no chance on their own. It is creating something greater than the sum of the parts that marks out the great rock bands, no matter what genre they operate in.

Instruments and Equipment

The guitar and amplifier you choose will combine with your own playing style to produce your 'sound'. It is therefore important to select the gear that suits your aim.

First to consider is the two types of guitar pickup, each with a very different but distinctive sound. The straightforward single-coil pickup as used by the Fender Stratocaster has a thin, trebly output in comparison to the humbucker favoured by Gibson-type guitars. Humbuckers have a thicker tone which is quite different to a

single coil pickup, so many modern guitars feature both to give a wider variety of sounds.

The tremolo arm, also called 'whammy bar' – or vibrato unit, to give it a more accurate name – is an optional extra on many guitar makes and lets you change string tension, and thus pitch, up or down by pulling or pushing as you play.

Even the most expensive electric guitar will only sound as good as the amp it is played through, so investing in the less pose-worthy side of the equation is well worth it. Famous makes used by rockers through the ages include Marshall, Fender, Vox and Mesa Boogie – but there are many more.

Valve or 'tube'-based amplification was standard until the Sixties, but transistorized (solid state) amplification is now the norm as it wins out in terms of cheapness and reliability (practice amps such as that below offer good sound without the screeching volume). However, more expensive valve amps will give you a sound that is richer and warmer. A compromise is offered by 'modelling' amps, a recent innovation that can approximate the sound of classic valve amps like the Marshall or Vox AC30.

The AC30 is one of many so-called combos. Short for combination, this is an amplifier and speaker(s) in one portable package; 90 per cent of guitarists will start off with one of these. But the ultimate 'rock rig' is a '4 x 12' (four 12-inch speakers in a cabinet) with a powerful separate amplifier on top – not as easy to transport if you are not relying on an army of roadies! An amplifier with growth potential will have at least 3-band EQ (equalization, i.e. bass, mid, and treble tone controls), two channels that can be plugged into, a 'clean' and a 'dirty' (overdrive), and maybe the option of a footswitch to change between them in mid-song.

Effects add colour and variety to the sound. Reverb and possibly chorus are the most useful, but any metal/hard rock guitarist worth their salt will have

an overdrive pedal to beef up their solos. Also, wah-wah, as used by Jimi Hendrix and many others since, can add emotion to your playing.

Musical Language and Characteristics

Perhaps the easiest way to divide today's rock scene is to say that some of the music is meant to make you feel good, and some is meant to be unsettling, even hard on the ear. This of course explains why Velvet Revolver sell more records than doom metal favourites Electric Wizard – but the fact that you are not on the radio does not debar you from either credibility or a loyal following.

The pentatonic guitar scale is the building block from which rock is constructed. A pentatonic is a musical scale with five pitches per octave. The major guitar scale corresponds to the Ionian mode in the modal system and is the 'happy-sounding' scale, while the minor guitar scale, the basic 'sad-sounding' scale, corresponds with the Aeolian mode.

You can use the minor scale over certain major chord progressions if you want a bluesy sound. When it comes to progressions that are based on power chords, the easiest way to figure out whether to use major pentatonic or minor pentatonic is by ear. If one does not sound right, try the other one and nine times out of 10, it will work perfectly. If both will work, you can mix and match in the same solo.

All scales are based on patterns on the fretboard, and are transposable. For example an A-minor pentatonic scale in the fifth position will become a B-flat pentatonic minor scale simply by moving that pattern up one fret or step on the fretboard. But the effect of what the guitarist is playing, be it a solo or a riff, is very much dependent on what is framing it in terms of music and percussion – quite apart from any vocal contribution. It is these contrasts that make the different rock genres so distinctive. It also means that guitar skills gained in one genre will be transferable to another.

Major pentatonic scale

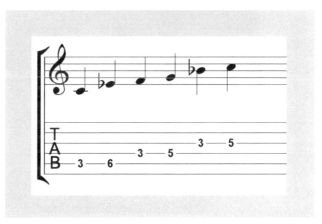

Minor pentatonic scale

Getting Ready to Play

Getting the Look

They say that image is half the battle in music, and the rock arena is no exception. It is important for a band to agree their visual identity long before they set foot on stage – too late arguing about these things in the pre-gig dressing room. Whether you take your sartorial cues from other bands in your chosen musical arena or dare to be different, the important thing is to look like you belong on the same stage.

Leather is popular – the perennial biker's jacket and/or trousers have always been staples of hard rockers since the late Sixties. Military chic can be added by means of a bullet belt, while Motörhead were hugely influential in the late Seventies by allying punk flair to the mix. Their 'death's head' T-shirt has become a fashion item in its own right. Spandex, the stretchy fabric beloved of Eighties bands like Saxon and Skid Row, is now usually used for ironic effect if at all.

Hair is an obvious way to express your individuality or your adherence to a musical creed. Headbands, like Spandex, are unashamedly retro, but if you cannot make your mind up take the easy option and wear a hat!

The Right Attitude

Playing in front of a live audience is something that does not come naturally to most of us. That is why the majority of guitarists never make it out of their bedroom. Exposing yourself to possible embarrassment and ridicule if you fall flat on your face is not an easy decision, but once you have heard the appreciation of an audience for a musical achievement then the effect is stronger than any drink or drug.

Talking of which, it is unwise to over-indulge before taking the stage. True, alcohol will help you lose your inhibitions but you can also lose your ability both to play and interact with your fellow musicians. Whether you are playing for love or money, your audience has come to see you do the best you can – the time to celebrate is when it is all over.

If you have a natural exhibitionist in the band, they would be the logical frontman, whether singing 'solo' or contributing guitar. Equally, the best guitarist should be given the opportunity to show off their talents – but it is well worth coaching the less extrovert band members to grab their share of the spotlight. Let a rhythm guitar player take one or two solos and it gives those numbers a different dimension, as well as encouraging him to come out of his shell.

Above all, remember you are there to enjoy yourselves – and if you do, chances are you will entertain your audience.

Tuning

Tuning is something best done in the dressing room before you hit the stage. Digital tuners are now within the financial reach of everyone, and are a reliable way to make sure your music will sound as intended. Note, however, that differences in temperature and humidity can affect tuning, so a floor-mounted tuner should be an essential part of your pedal board. This can also let you check your tuning between songs without being heard by the audience.

Modified tunings have been a part of hard rock since Jimmy Page introduced them to Led Zeppelin's music back in the late Sixties. An open tuning is one where the guitar is tuned so that a chord is achieved without fretting any of the strings. Other chords may then be played by simply barring a fret or through use of a slide.

Drop D is the most common modified tuning in modern rock, and was particularly favoured by 'grunge' bands. Drop D enables the guitarist to play a whole tone lower than in standard tuning, giving a deeper, fuller sound. The only difference between Drop D and standard tuning is that you lower (drop) the sixth (heaviest) string from an E down to a D. This also has the effect of making the bottom three strings (thickest) a power chord without a major or minor.

Some bands down-tune a semitone in order to get a weightier sound or compensate for the vocal range of their singer. This means the E string will now be tuned to E flat, and the others will be flattened likewise to remain in relative tune to their fellows. Some bands – Tool, Limp Bizkit and Queens of the Stone Age – have been known to go even further. Down-tuning is not exclusively for metal bands; Hendrix and Stevie Ray Vaughan were known to drop a semitone.

Warming Up

There's no way an athlete would set foot on a running track or footballer on a football pitch without having physically prepared themselves. Exercises are the best way to ensure your hands are ready to rock, and most guitarists have their own favourites. They can also help you avoid pain and suffering further down the line: tendonitis, carpal tunnel syndrome or other repetitive stress injuries are among the problems lying in wait for the unwary.

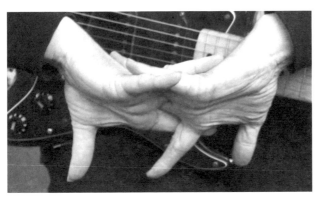

Hand stretch

Finger stretch

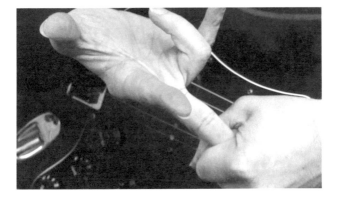

You should try to put aside at least a quarter of an hour before playing to warm up. And the first part of the process should be accomplished without even taking your instrument out of its case. Stretches for your wrists, hands and fingers should precede any actual playing. Reaching your left hand across your body, bend your right hand back to make a 90-degree angle. Gently bend a little beyond that 90-degree position then repeat, switching hands. Then, bend back each finger of each hand one at a time, just far enough to get a good stretch. Then repeat, this time bending back two side-by-side fingers at a time. Repeat the process three or four times.

After all this foreplay, you are finally allowed to pick up your instrument! Playing scales or arpeggios are favourite warm-ups, starting slow and speeding up. Incorporate hammer-ons and pull-offs and vary your picking patterns. You will find that by doing these exercises, however repetitive and uncreative they may seem, you gain in speed and dexterity. As with so many other aspects of guitar playing, practice makes perfect.

Techniques

How to Use Plectrums and Strings

Most guitarists use a plastic plectrum to attack the strings, and these range in thickness from light gauge (around .44 millimetres) to heavy (one millimetre) and beyond. The thinner ones are ideal for strumming chords, while the thicker will prove more effective for riffs and single-string solos. Buy a selection to see which suits your playing style.

We examine individual picking styles later on in this book, but it is important to avoid anchoring your picking

(right) hand either on the body or the strings as you lose flexibility. Let it float lightly above the strings instead. Another alternative is to play with your fingers instead of a pick. This makes for more response and sensitivity, say those who use the method.

While the plectrum you use will affect the sound achieved, so will the gauge of the strings it is playing. An extra light set of strings will generally start from a .010 and run through to a .047, while heavy might be .014 to .059 with light and medium gauges in-between. Thicker strings provide better tone and are more suited to rock riffs but are harder

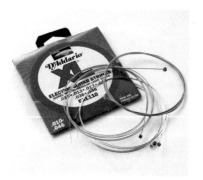

to play, while lighter strings are best for lead guitarists who want to bend notes. Famous brand names include D'Addario, Fender and Dean Markley.

Playing a Lead Solo

A lead guitar solo will usually involve playing single strings at a time rather than the multiple-string technique used for chords. Character can be added by the use of techniques like hammer-ons and pull-offs; these are also known as slurs, and create a smoother sound between notes rather like a saxophone player playing multiple notes with a single breath.

To hammer-on, a second note is sounded by hammering another finger onto the same string at a higher fret than the one first played. Pull-offs are the opposite, but note that your left-hand finger

Solo techniques 1: alternating pull offs.

Solo techniques 2: hammer on and off, alternating the string – steps 1 to 4.

needs to almost pluck the fretted string as it is removed to obtain the desired volume and effect. Other techniques to consider include varying your timing as well as the notes themselves, sustaining notes where they sound good, and creating swells using the volume control on your guitar. Turning your volume down, hammering-on a note and raising the volume creates an interesting effect. Then there's vibrato and string bending,

Solo techniques 3: fast pull off on single string.

Solo techniques 4: string bend, two-finger style!

respectively using the fingers to move the string along its length to make a wobbling sound or up and down to create less subtle changes.

The Pentatonic is the standard scale used in rock, but a safe way to proceed is to ascertain the key of the song and start your solo at the root note. The A pentatonic scale, for instance, starts at the fifth fret on the lowest E string.

Solo techniques 5: slide from high note to lower note using heavy sustain.

Power Chords

Most heavy rock songs are based around power chords made up of the root and fifth notes. The interval that makes a chord major or minor is its 'third' – major chords have a major third, minor chords have a minor third – but power chords are different. They lack a third completely. This makes them sound much more powerful when played through a distorted amp. An example of a power chord is A, whose root note is A, fifth is E and octave A.

Barre chords enable chord shapes to be moved up and down the fretboard, retaining their original major or minor quality but changing pitch and name. The index finger spans all six strings, while the others form the familiar shapes in front of it as if it were the nut at the peghead end of the fretboard. For example, moving the E shape up a fret turns it into F. The concept is relatively simple, but can be difficult for the beginner to master.

To make an effective barre or power chord, your index finger must press down hard enough so all the strings ring out clearly; your thumb should be directly behind your index at the back of the neck to apply maximum force.

All these chords sound best when played through a mildly overdriven amp.

Shredding Techniques

The technique known as sweep picking involves matching a 'sweeping' motion of the pick in the right hand to produce a fast and fluid series of notes. With the left (fretting) hand operating a matching technique, both combine to achieve the desired effect.

Alternate picking is a term describing the most common method of playing with a plectrum, in which downward and upward picking strokes alternate. (This is known as tremolo picking when performed on a single note at a high speed.) The continuous down-up or up-down motion of the picking hand, even when not picking a note, means an up-beat note will always be played with an upward stroke, while the down-beats are always played with downward strokes. This allows hammer-ons and pull-offs to be incorporated.

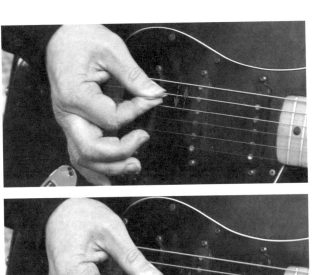

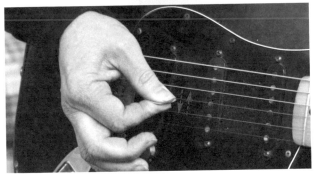

Tapping means using the fingers of one hand to 'tap' the strings against the fingerboard, thus sounding legato notes. The technique usually incorporates pull-offs or hammer-ons, the fingers of the left (fretting) hand playing a sequence of notes in sync with the tapping hand. Eddie Van Halen's playing on 'Eruption' from his band's first album paved the way for guitarists in the Eighties to experiment with this.

String skipping, as the name implies, sees a string skipped during a riff for effect rather than the guitarist using adjacent strings as is usual.

Palm Muting

Palm muting is a guitar technique widely used in hard rock, heavy metal and particularly thrash, speed and death metal, in which the side or heel of the hand (not the palm, confusingly) muffles the strings slightly while they are being picked. If part of the song is played in this way, the part that is played conventionally will seem louder and more aggressive by comparison. Megadeth, Slayer, Metallica, Pantera and Anthrax were among the technique's pioneers.

The key is to mute the notes only slightly, not so much that they cannot be heard. Only practice will show how much pressure you need to

Muting with the heel of the hand.

apply with the heel of your picking hand. A very even, controlled sound is the aim. Once you have mastered the technique, degrees of muting can be employed from light, in other words letting the notes clearly be heard, through to the almost percussive effect of heavy palm muting.

In general, the nearer your muting hand is to the guitar bridge the more effective it will be, while fast alternate picking creates a driving feel. Applying effects will accentuate the technique: distortion is effective, while a wah-wah pedal produces a particularly vicious result.

Muting with the side of the hand.

Pinch Harmonics

A harmonic is the bell-like tone you get by damping
specific frets on the guitar's fingerboard, and can
provide some very useful effects. The main sound
you hear when you strike a guitar string is known
as the fundamental, and comes from the string
vibrating along its full length between bridge and
nut. But other tones can also be heard, resulting
from shorter frequencies vibrating along different
parts of the string. These are known as harmonics,
or overtones, and their combination with the

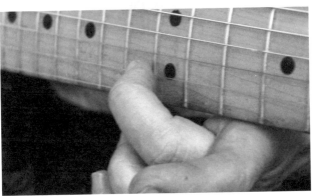

Harmonic technique 1: Finger rests lightly on the string, not pushing down.

Harmonic technique 2: The forefinger rests lightly on the note, while the index finger picks the same string. This allows the left hand to play notes other than the octaves above the open string harmonics.

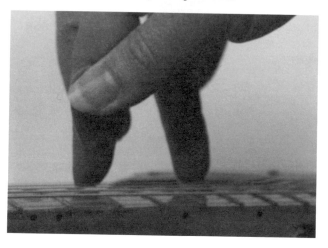

fundamental creates the tonal characteristics of the note produced.

The simplest harmonics can be produced by fretting a note with your left hand, then picking the string 12 frets (one octave) further up the neck. While picking, let your thumb touch the string just after the pick hits it, then immediately remove it. The pick will make the note play, while your thumb should mute the fundamental, leaving the harmonic. Pinch harmonics (and artificial harmonics) can also be found at other points by dividing the string into thirds or fourths.

Using your bridge pickup will usually give you a better result, but you can experiment by moving your picking spot towards the neck until you hear the 'ping'. This technique can be accentuated by using a distorted guitar sound, while employing a whammy bar to suddenly lower the pinched notes is also effective.

Rhythm Guitar

The term 'rhythm guitar' describes a style of playing where you are almost as much a percussionist as a guitarist. You are providing the musical canvas on which the vocals and lead guitar can weave their patterns – but without the canvas their work would be impossible, so the role of rhythm guitar is by no means secondary or inferior. Rhythm guitarists are often also singers, but not exclusively: AC/DC's Malcolm Young and Aerosmith's Brad Whitford are among the specialist rhythm merchants.

As a rhythm player, you use your plectrum to pick either basic riffs, strum all six strings, or combinations of both. In metal music, you can expect to be asked to play complex sequences consisting of a combination of chords, single notes and palm-muted parts, while more technical bands may expect riffs which demand lead guitar techniques.

If your role is dedicated rhythm guitarist you may want to choose equipment that 'fattens' your sound, for example humbucking pickups and valve (or valve emulating) amplification. Strings, too, may benefit from being heavier gauge than the lead guitar. It is clearly crucial to have a good sense of timing, so practise along with recordings or use a metronome.

Distortion & Feedback

Distortion and feedback are cornerstones of hard rock and heavy metal. Distortion originally came from running guitar amplifiers at excessive volumes, while the higher-pitched feedback is the noise that happens when a microphone (or guitar pickup) amplifies a sound it picks up and creates a 'loop' which feeds back on itself.

Eric Clapton brought distortion into rock music when recording with John Mayall's Bluesbreakers in 1966. By bringing his stage amplification into the studio, where smaller amps were more usually found, he created a precedent, and by the time Jimi Hendrix hit the recording scene months later anything went in the guitar department.

Distortion is most easily and predictably achieved today through use of an effects pedal like the Boss DS1 – over 20 years old but still a standard today. Another is the Tubescreamer from Ibanez, a widely-imitated pedal adding a vacuum tube-like distortion sound using transistors. The Marshall

Bluesbreaker is another market leader named in homage to Clapton. A distortion pedal is not a substitute for a good amp, but amp distortion will not provide the 'on demand' effect provided by a good distortion pedal.

Since the Seventies, many guitar amplifiers have included an overdrive circuit, to provide a real or simulated tube overdrive sound alongside the normal 'clean' input. This may range from a slight added 'growl' or 'edge', with some increase in sustain, up to a thick, distorted fuzzy sound.

Feedback is achieved by holding your guitar close to your speaker(s) and letting it pick up and amplify the output to obtain that distinctive 'ringing' sound. Once achieved, the distance from and direction in which you move from your stack or combo will determine the volume and strength of the effect.

The Music
Using the Examples

The examples are divided by type of music and indicated by the tabs at the edge of each page. Each type is given a series of generic examples for lead play, rhythm and riffs. Both notation and tab is provided, although chord boxes are given where appropriate.

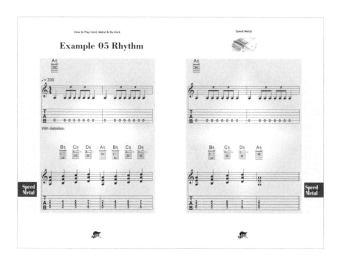

Black Metal

Black Metal

Black metal owes its existence to thrash. The term 'black metal' was borrowed from a Venom album title in 1982 and Swedish band Bathory, formed in 1983, would begin a long Scandinavian association with the genre.

Musically, screamed vocals and fast and distorted metallic guitars – as in thrash – were used to create an uneasy atmosphere, incorporating minor, sometimes diminished chords. Chromatics were often shifted up and down by semitones from a central tonic. Some bands employed drum machines instead of a human drummer, while recordings were often of a deliberate low quality to add to their cult appeal.

As the Nineties approached bands like Darkthrone and Mayhem from Norway began a second wave of black metal, emphasizing unusual song structures which often ignored conventional verse-chorus patterns and favoured repeated instrumental sections. Cradle of Filth and Dimmu Borgir are among the leading black metal bands of recent years.

Black Metal

Example 01 Lead

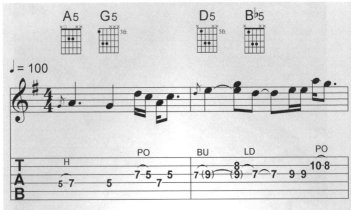

With distortion.
Drop all strings by 1½ tones.

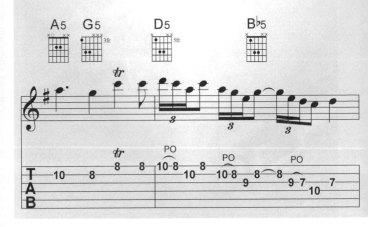

Black Metal

Example 02 Lead

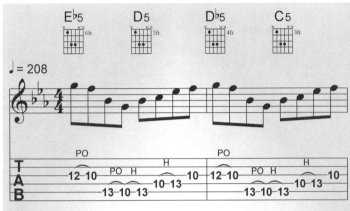

With distortion.
Drop all strings by 1½ tones.

**Black
Metal**

Example 03 Lead

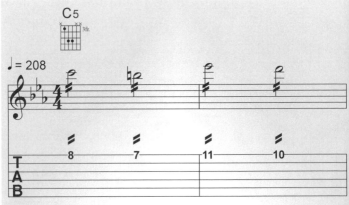

Constant tremolo picking with distortion.
Drop all strings by 1½ tones.

Example 04 Lead

Drop all strings by 1½ tones.

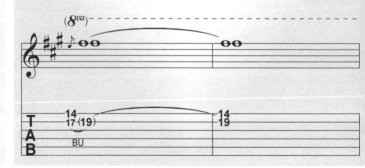

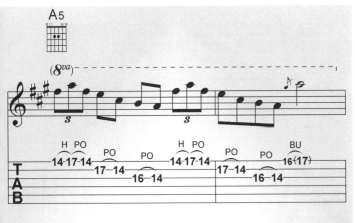

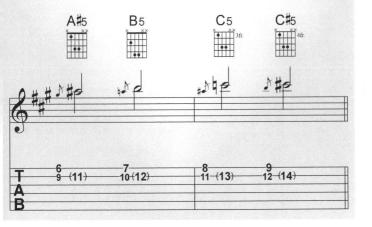

Example 05 Rhythm

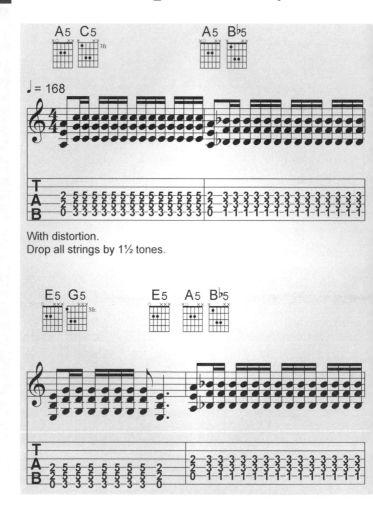

With distortion.
Drop all strings by 1½ tones.

Example 06 Rhythm

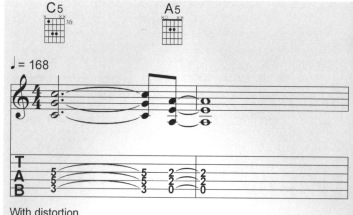

With distortion.
Drop all strings by 1½ tones.

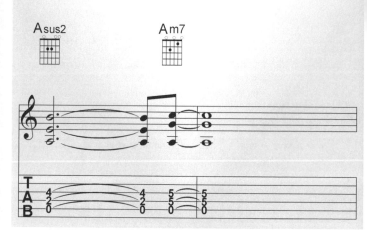

Black Metal

Example 07 Rhythm

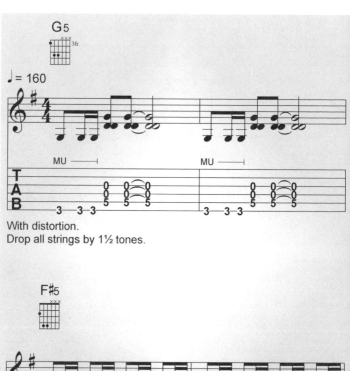

With distortion.
Drop all strings by 1½ tones.

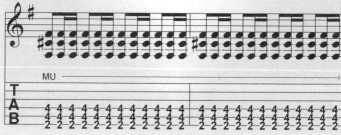

Example 08 Rhythm

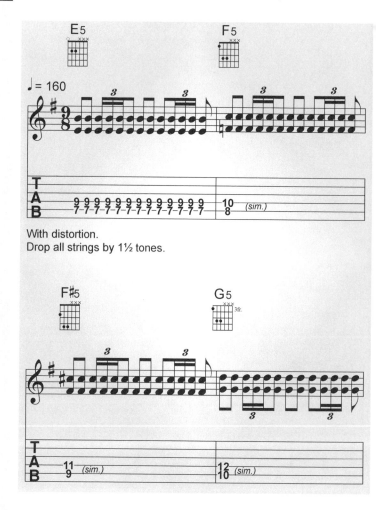

With distortion.
Drop all strings by 1½ tones.

Black Metal

**Black
Metal**

Example 09 Riff

Let notes ring where possible throughout.

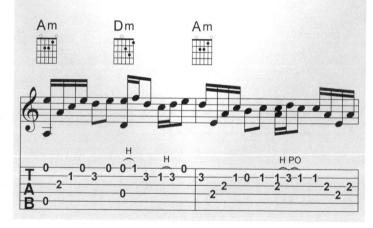

Black Metal

Example 10 Riff

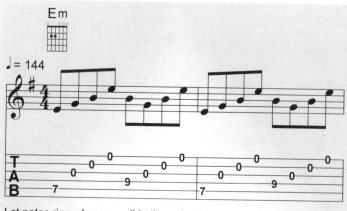

Let notes ring where possible throughout.

Example 11 Riff

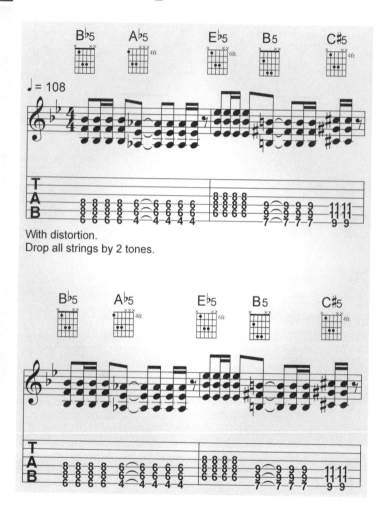

With distortion.
Drop all strings by 2 tones.

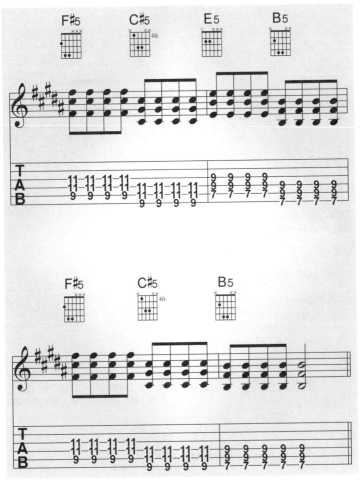

Example 12 Riff

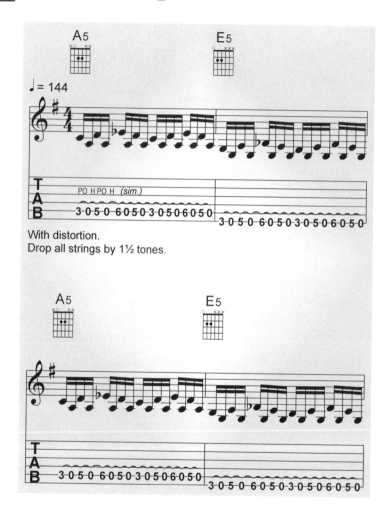

With distortion.
Drop all strings by 1½ tones.

Black Metal

Death Metal

The easiest way to separate death metal from black metal is not so much through the guitar-playing but the vocals: singers in death metal bands favour a lower, more guttural delivery, while their voices will often be treated with effects such as reverberation to make a more threatening sound.

Lyrically, the genre preaches the inevitability of death and nihilism rules. Death metal's musical structure is equally grim. The previously mentioned guttural, chanted vocals overlay sledgehammer rhythms, muted picking, tremolo strumming of single strings, intricate riffs and power chords – all combining to hammer home the bleak lyrical message. Slayer and Possessed were among death metal's pioneers, creating the sub-genre from thrash metal in the mid Eighties. The 1984 compilation 'Death Metal', released by Noise Records, was the first recorded use of the name, while the aptly named Suicide are among today's death metal front-runners.

Example 01 Lead

Death Metal

N.C. throughout.

Drop all strings by 1½ tones.

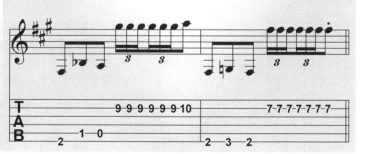

Example 02 Lead

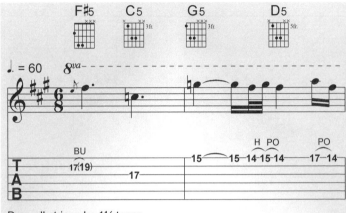

Drop all strings by 1½ tones.

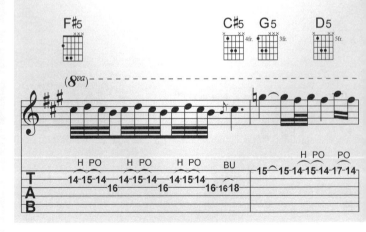

Death Metal

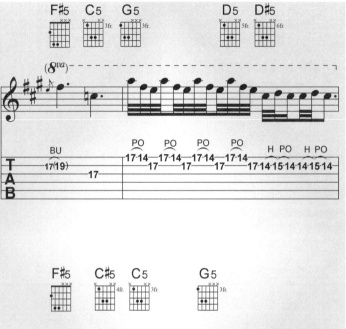

Example 03 Lead

With distortion.
Drop all strings by 1 tone.

Death Metal

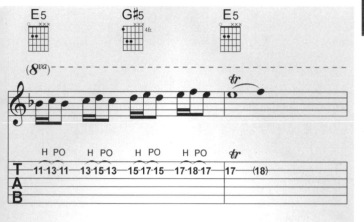

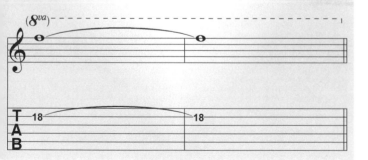

Example 04 Lead

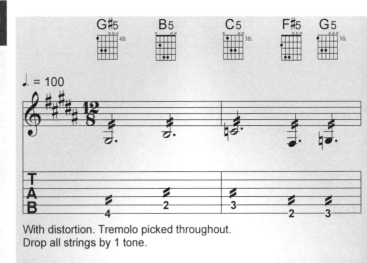

With distortion. Tremolo picked throughout.
Drop all strings by 1 tone.

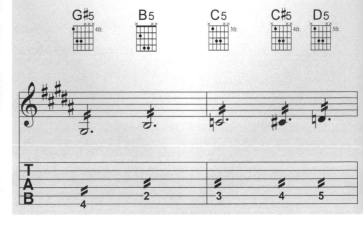

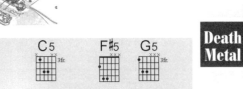

Example 05 Rhythm

Death Metal

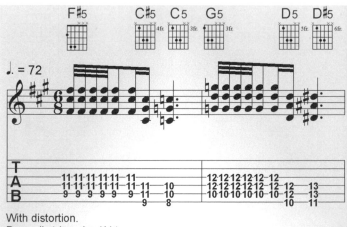

With distortion.
Drop all strings by 1½ tones.

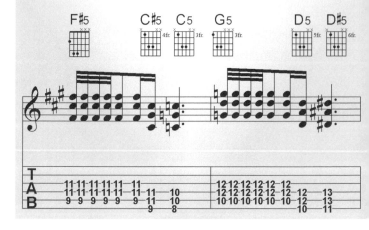

Death Metal

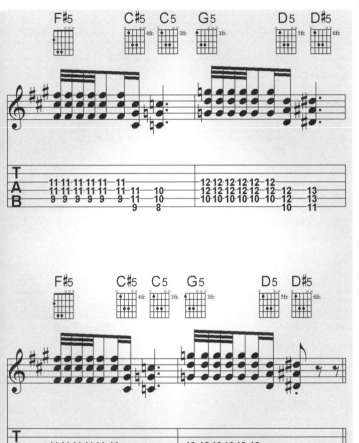

Example 06 Rhythm

**Death
Metal**

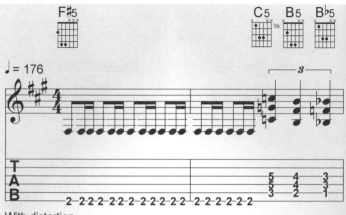

With distortion.
Drop all strings by 1½ tones.

Death Metal

Example 07 Rhythm

Death Metal

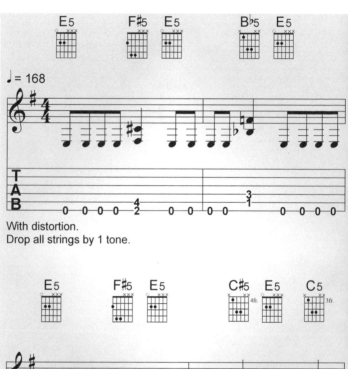

With distortion.
Drop all strings by 1 tone.

Death Metal

Example 08 Rhythm

With distortion.
Drop all strings by 1 tone.

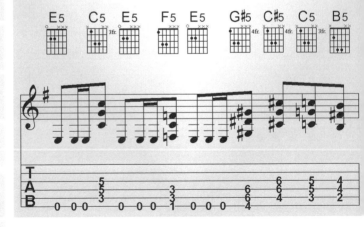

Death Metal

Example 09 Riff

Death Metal

With distortion.
Drop all strings by 1½ tones.

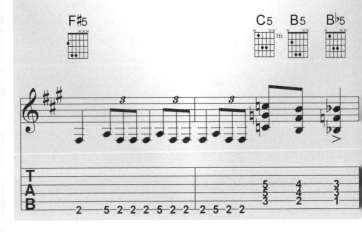

Example 10 Riff

Death Metal

Tremolo picking with distortion.
Drop all strings by 1½ tones.

Death Metal

Example 11 Riff

Death Metal

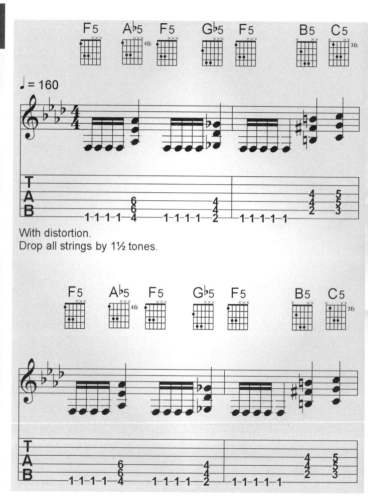

With distortion.
Drop all strings by 1½ tones.

Death Metal

Death Metal

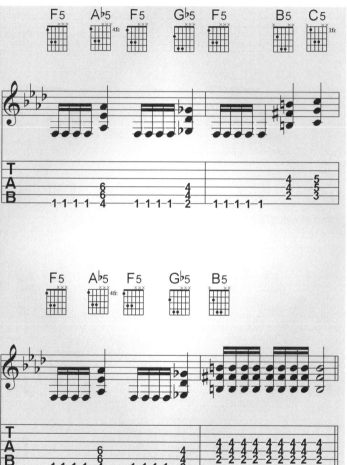

105

Example 12 Riff

Death Metal

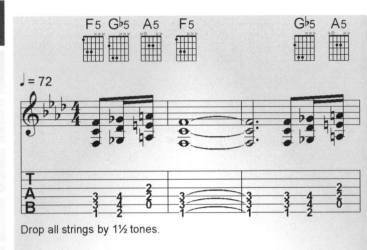

Drop all strings by 1½ tones.

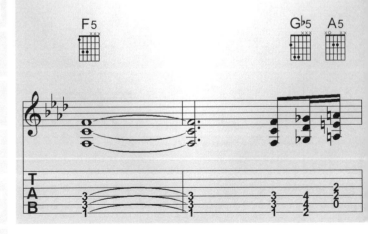

Death Metal

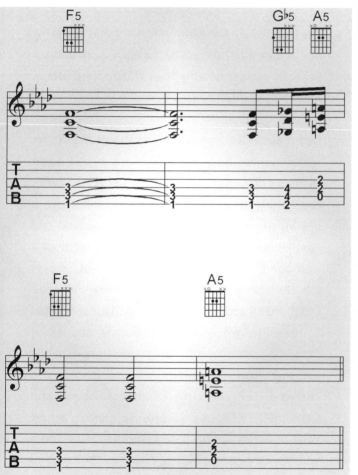

Doom Metal

The Eighties phenomenon of doom metal was fairly and squarely influenced by the early work of Black Sabbath – most notably their classic third album *Master Of Reality*, released in 1971.

Doom metal is both heavier and slower than other metal genres and often features tuned-down instruments. As the name suggests, lyrics concentrate on despair and misery and evoke a pessimistic atmosphere. Witchfinder General and Candlemass were pioneers, but the formation of a new band, Cathedral, by ex Napalm Death singer Lee Dorrian gave the movement new impetus. Death metal and doom metal in particular merged at the edges when bands like Sorrow and (early) Paradise Lost slowed down the tempo, while extreme and even hardcore influences also surfaced. Lee Dorrian's label Rise Above and Germany's Hellhound Records supported a new wave of bands like Solitude Aeturnus, Count Raven and the Obsessed. Leading doom metal bands of today include Electric Wizard and Orodruin.

Example 01 Lead

Doom Metal

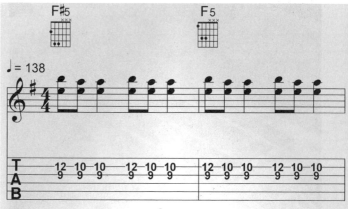

With distortion.
6th string to D. Drop all strings by 1 tone.

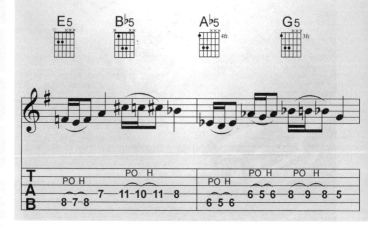

Doom Metal

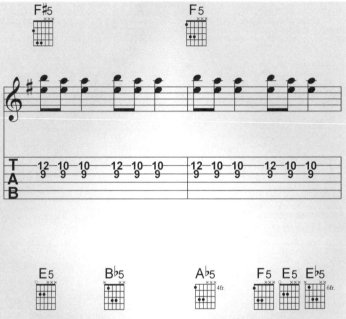

Example 02 Lead

Doom Metal

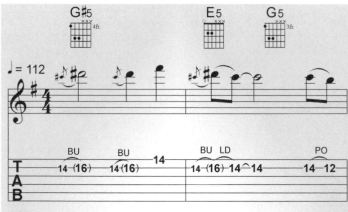

With distortion.
6th string to D. Drop all strings by 1 tone.

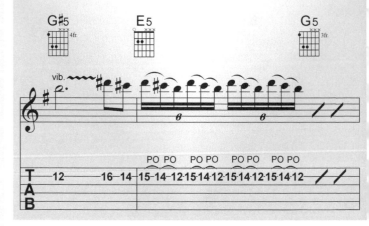

Doom Metal

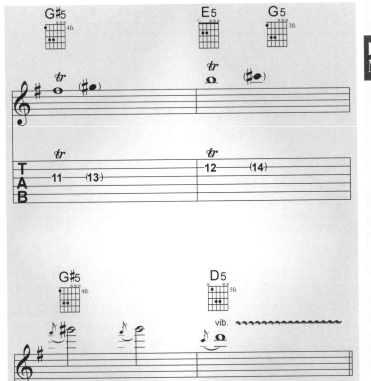

Example 03 Lead

Doom Metal

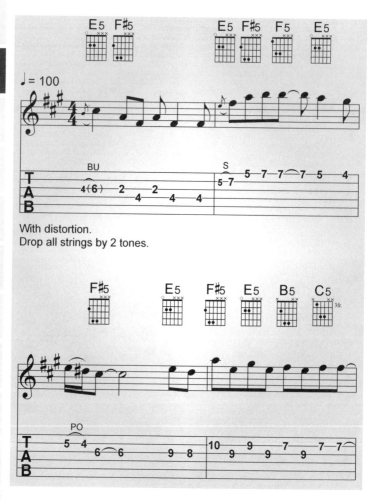

With distortion.
Drop all strings by 2 tones.

Doom Metal

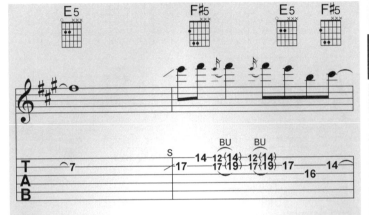

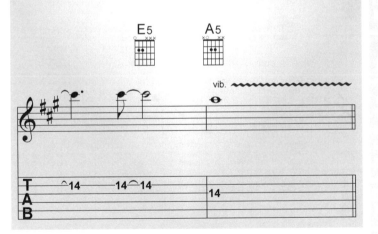

Example 04 Lead

Doom Metal

With distortion.

Doom Metal

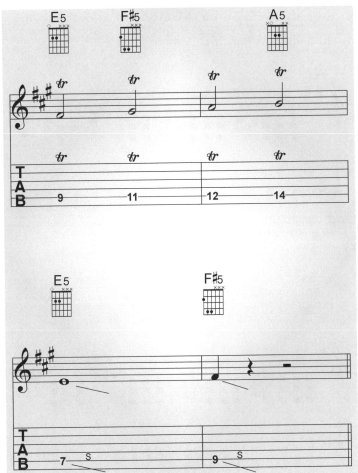

Example 05 Rhythm

Doom Metal

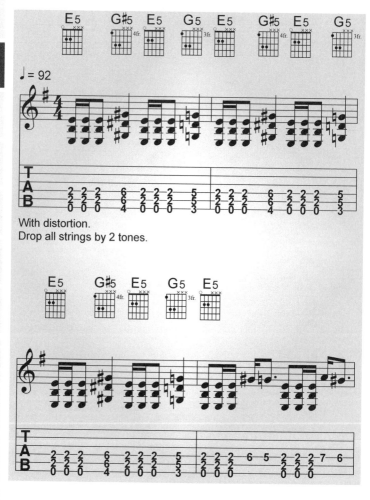

With distortion.
Drop all strings by 2 tones.

Doom Metal

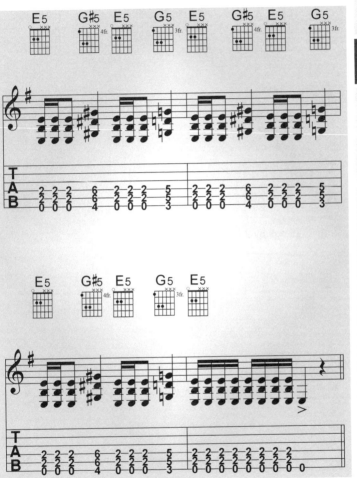

Example 06 Rhythm

Doom Metal

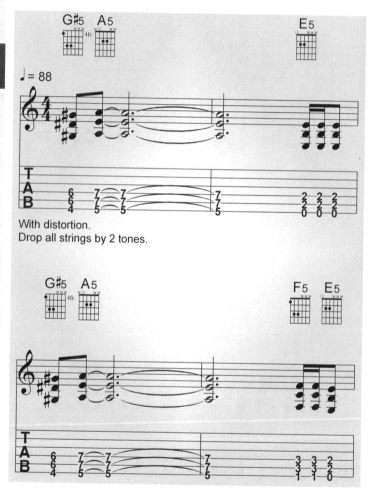

With distortion.
Drop all strings by 2 tones.

Doom Metal

Example 07 Rhythm

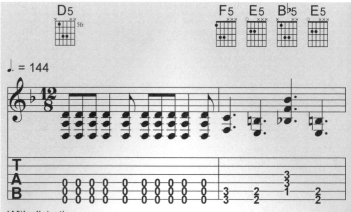

With distortion.
6th string to D. Drop all strings by 1 tone.

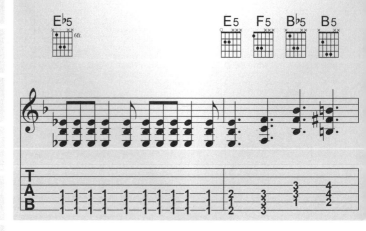

Doom Metal

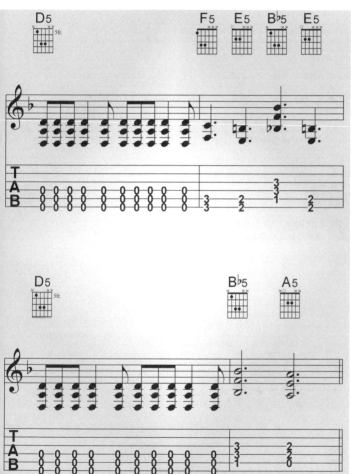

Example 08 Rhythm

Doom Metal

With distortion and palm muting.
6th string to D. Drop all strings by 1 tone.

Doom Metal

Example 09 Riff

Doom Metal

With distortion.
6th string to D. Drop all strings by 1 tone.

Doom Metal

Example 10 Riff

Doom Metal

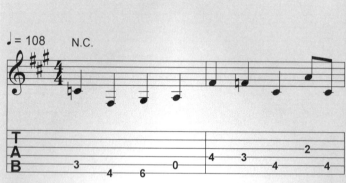

With distortion.
6th string to D. Drop all strings by 1 tone.

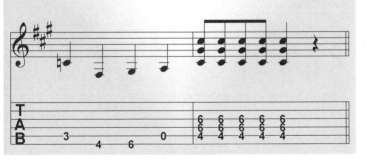

Example 11 Riff

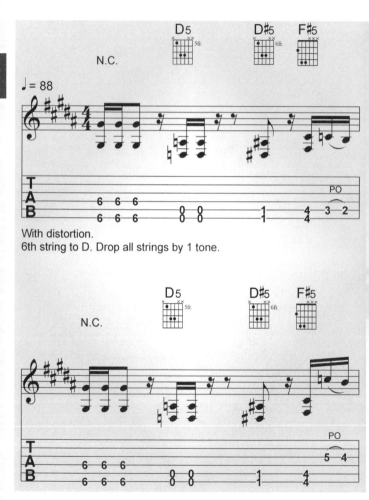

With distortion.
6th string to D. Drop all strings by 1 tone.

Doom Metal

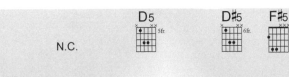

Example 12 Riff

Doom Metal

With distortion.
Drop all strings by 2 tones.

Doom Metal

Goth Rock

Goth Rock

The first gothic rock bands emerged from the new wave of the late Seventies and early Eighties and acquired their name as much for the presentation of their music as the music itself. Bands like Bauhaus, the Cure and the Damned used stage sets, makeup and clothing to augment their dark-themed output. *Sounds* music paper first coined the phrase gothic (or goth) rock in 1981, in reference to the band UK Decay. A wave of bands including the Sisters of Mercy, Fields of the Nephilim, Christian Death, the Mission and Mephisto Waltz found popularity, while the Cult, who started life as Southern Death Cult, used goth as a launch pad for more mainstream success.

Musically, goth places great emphasis on the bass, six-string guitar lines tending to be angular riffs and phrases rather than chords. The picking style is generally downward in direction, as it was with goth's punk predecessor. Minor keys and the Phrygian mode also predominate, while the main percussive drive is supplied by the snare drum.

Example 01 Lead

Goth Rock

Clean sound with delay.

Goth Rock

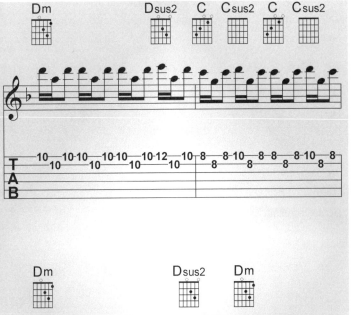

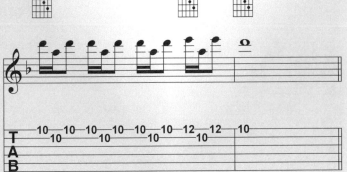

Example 02 Lead

Acoustic guitar.

Goth
Rock

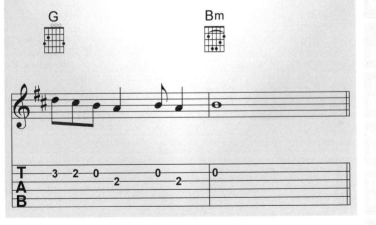

Example 03 Lead

Clean sound with delay.

Goth Rock

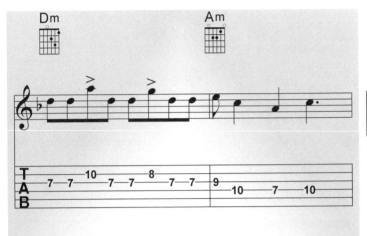

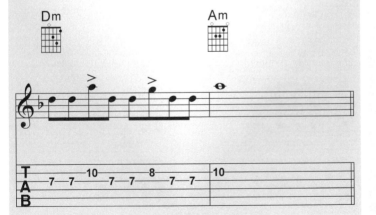

Example 04 Rhythm

Goth
Rock

With distortion.

Goth Rock

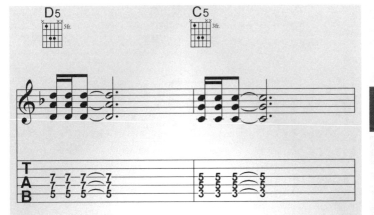

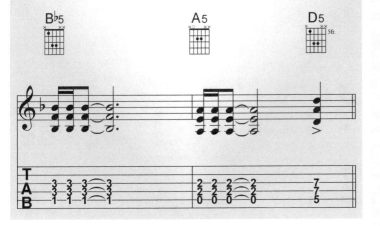

Example 05 Rhythm

Goth Rock

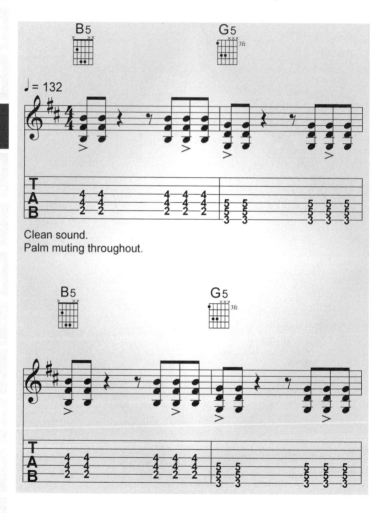

Clean sound.
Palm muting throughout.

Goth Rock

Example 06 Rhythm

Goth Rock

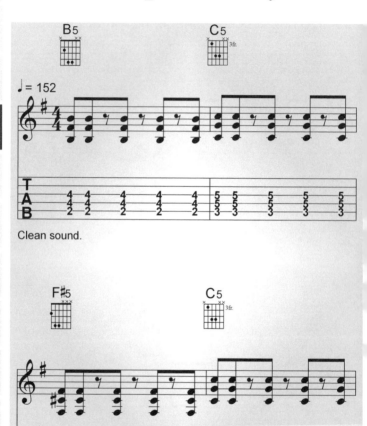

Clean sound.

Goth Rock

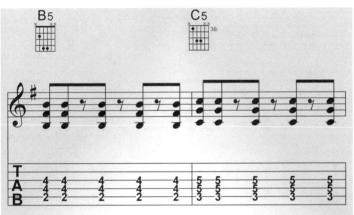

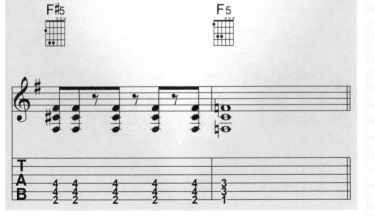

Example 07 Rhythm

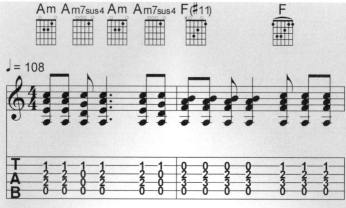

**Goth
Rock**

Clean sound with chorus.

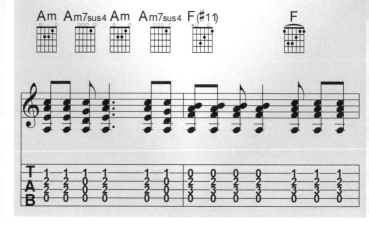

Goth Rock

Example 08 Rhythm

With chorus and delay.

Goth Rock

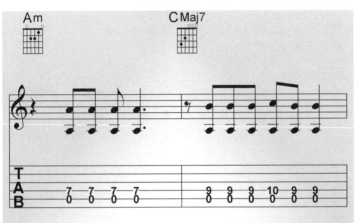

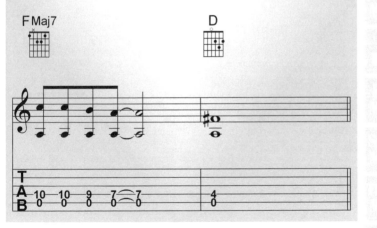

151

Example 09 Riff

Goth Rock

N.C.

♩ = 126   Let ring

With chorus and delay.

Goth Rock

Example 10 Riff

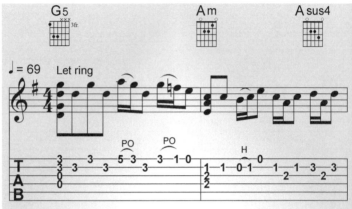

With overdrive and flanger.

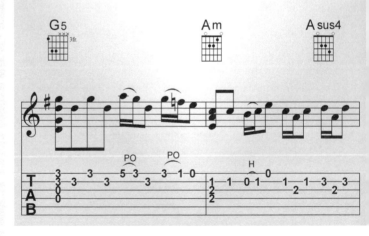

Goth Rock

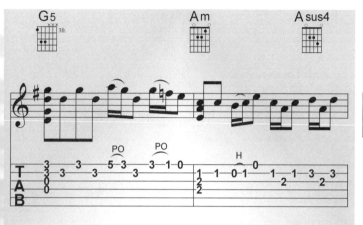

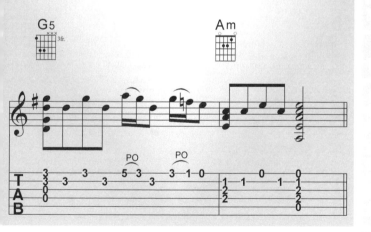

Goth
Rock

155

Example 11 Riff

Goth Rock

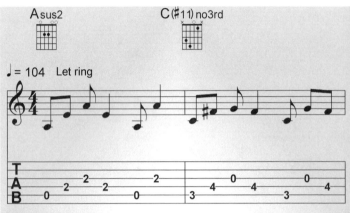

Clean sound with chorus.

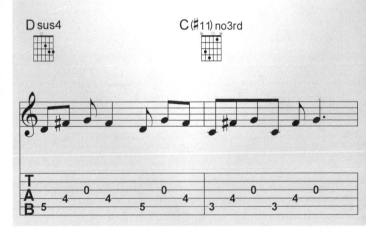

Goth Rock

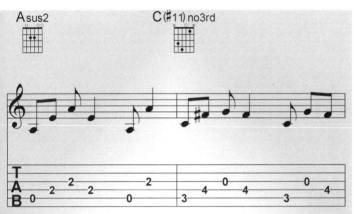

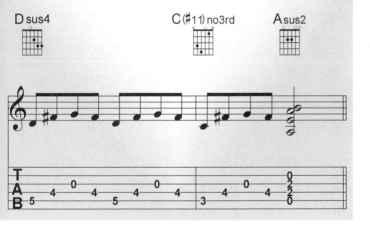

Example 12 Riff

Goth
Rock

Clean sound with chorus.

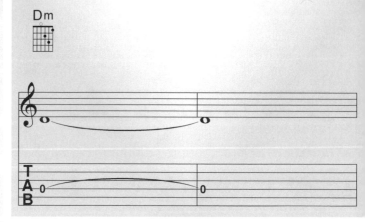

Goth Rock

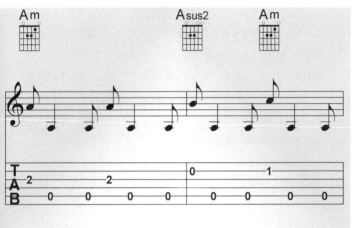

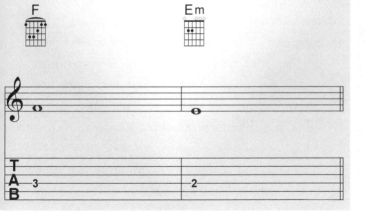

Grindcore

Grindcore fuses the harsh vocal style of death metal with high-energy hardcore punk riffing, using chromatic and counterpoint compositional techniques to create sounds intended to 'grind' against one another. It shares the punk genre's preference for fast songs and very fast drumming. Pioneer grindcore bands apart from Napalm Death include Nasum, Pig Destroyer and Mortician.

While 30–40 seconds is around the average song length, there also exists a format known as the microsong. Napalm Death's 'You Suffer', at just over one second long, is often credited as being the shortest song ever. There is also often humour in the lyrics – another punk tendency. And while it shares death metal's low-tuned guitars, blastbeats and double bass drums and growled vocals, its practitioners do not necessarily strive for excellent musicianship.

Discharge and Amebix were grindcore leaders in Britain, while America boasted the likes of Siege, and Repulsion.

Grind
Core

Example 01 Lead

With distortion.
Drop all strings by 1 semitone.

Grindcore

Example 02 Lead

Grind Core

With distortion.
Drop all strings by 1 semitone.

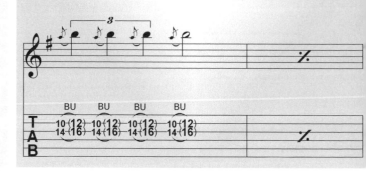

Grindcore

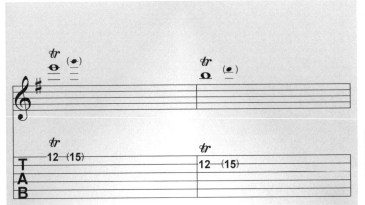

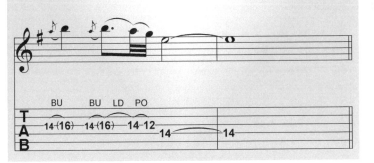

Example 03 Lead

With distortion.

Grind Core

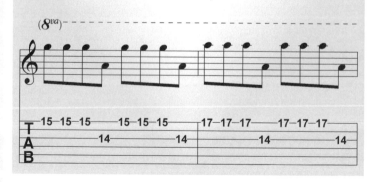

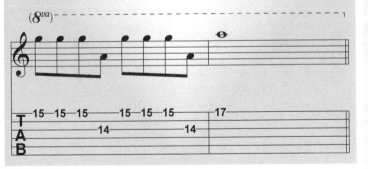

Example 04 Rhythm

Grind Core

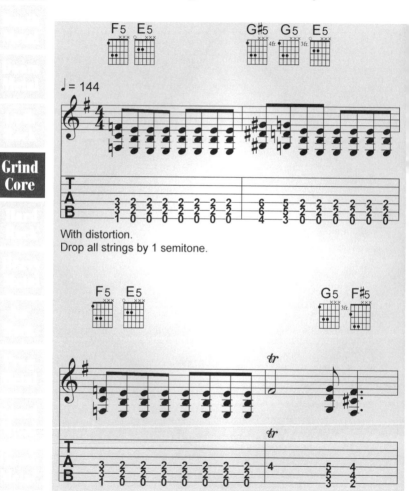

With distortion.
Drop all strings by 1 semitone.

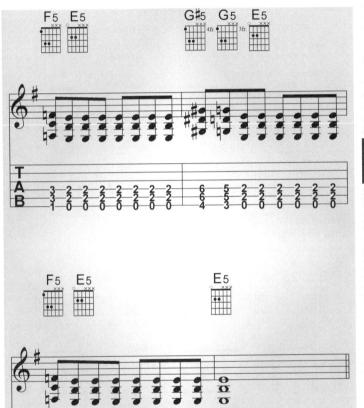

Grind
Core

Example 05 Rhythm

With distortion.
Drop all strings by 1 semitone.

Grindcore

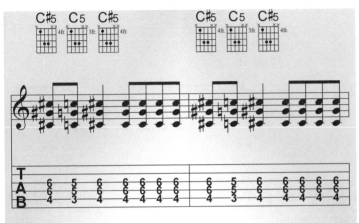

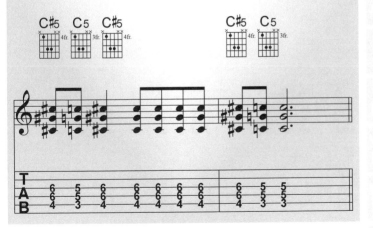

Example 06 Rhythm

Grind Core

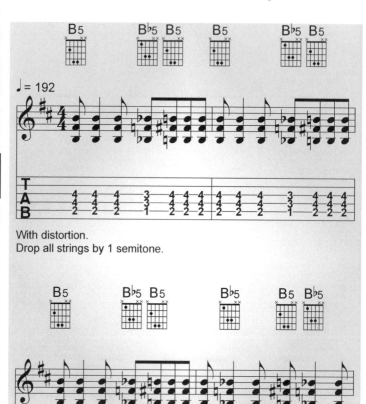

With distortion.
Drop all strings by 1 semitone.

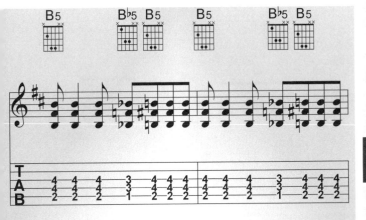

Grind
Core

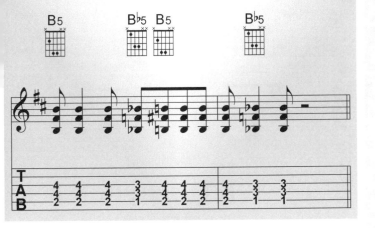

Example 07 Rhythm

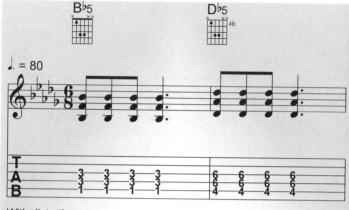

With distortion.
Drop all strings by 1 semitone.

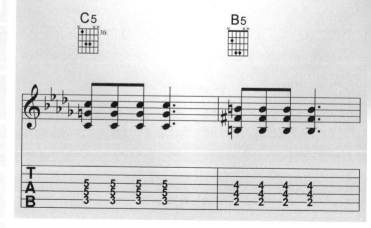

Grindcore

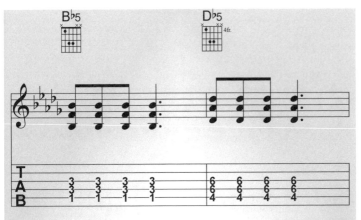

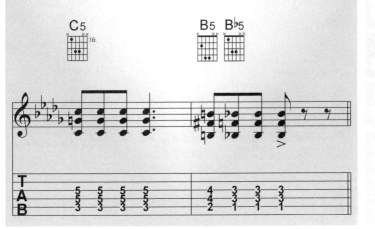

Example 08 Rhythm

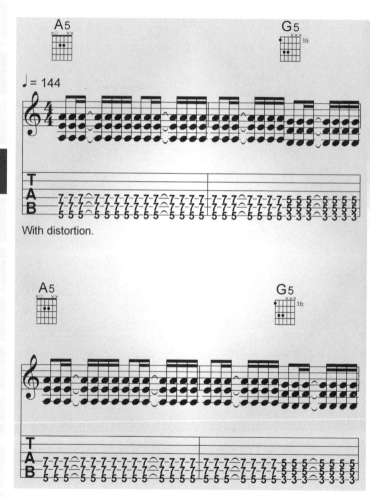

With distortion.

Grindcore

Example 09 Riff

Grind
Core

With distortion.
Drop all strings by 1 semitone.

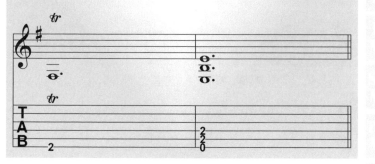

Example 10 Riff

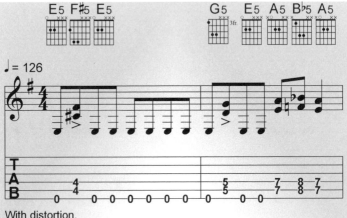

With distortion.
Drop all strings by 1 semitone.

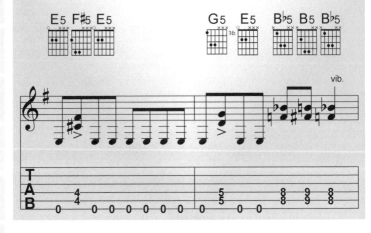

Grindcore

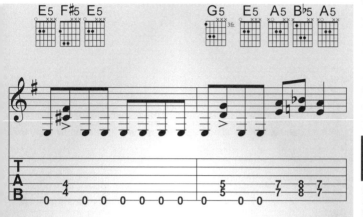

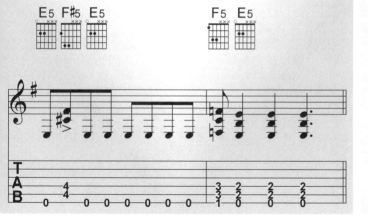

Grind
Core

Example 11 Riff

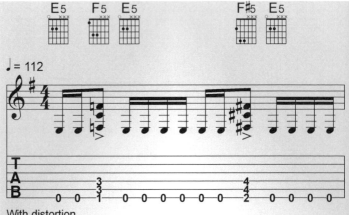

With distortion.
Drop all strings by 1 semitone.

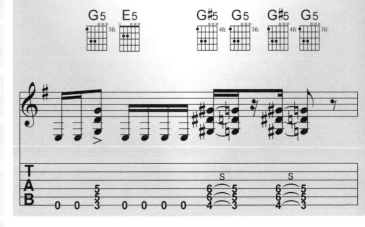

Grindcore

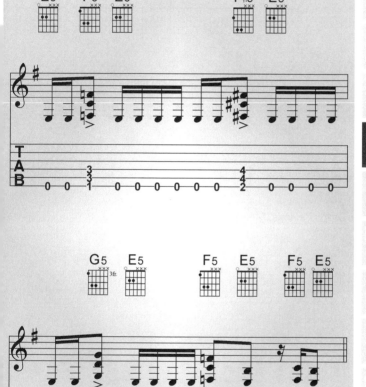

Indie
Metal

Death
Metal

Grind
Metal

Goth
Rock

**Grind
Core**

Hard
Rock

Heavy
Metal

Nu
Metal

Dark
Metal

Death
Metal

Dark
Metal

Metal

Example 12 Riff

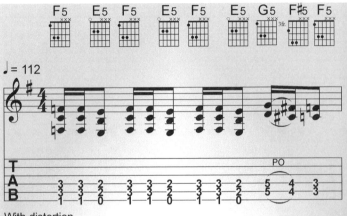

With distortion.
Drop all strings by 1 semitone.

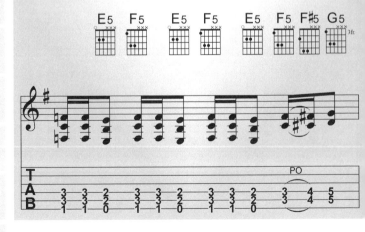

Grindcore

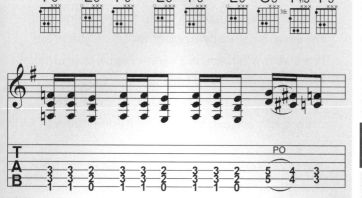

Hard Rock

The definition of hard rock can be a wide one, but the genre is generally accepted to have begun in the late Sixties when America's Frank Zappa, Doors, Jimi Hendrix and Vanilla Fudge set the tone for the Seventies with distorted guitars, slowed-down, druggy riffs and extravagant stage presentation.

Bands like Aerosmith that followed a few years later in their wake would not have considered themselves heavy metal, yet used amplified overdriven guitars as the basis of their sound and would happily have owned up to the 'hard rock' label. Black Sabbath, Led Zeppelin and Deep Purple are often considered to be both heavy metal and hard rock, whereas bands such as AC/DC, Aerosmith, Thin Lizzy, Guns N' Roses, Van Halen and Kiss are normally referred to as hard rock. Punk's links with hard rock were underlined by bands like Motörhead, who had a foot in both camps. Hard rock has the biggest crossover potential to the mainstream than any other form of rock, so there has been a tendency for bands to form and re-form as record labels bank on exploiting an existing fan base.

Hard Rock

Example 01 Lead

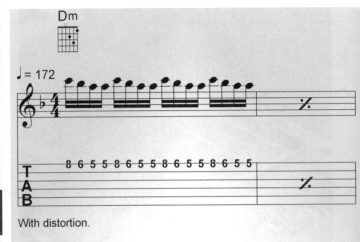

With distortion.

Hard Rock

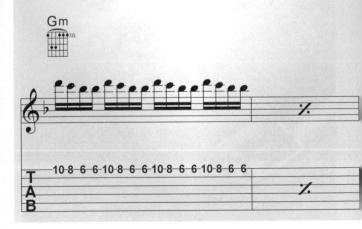

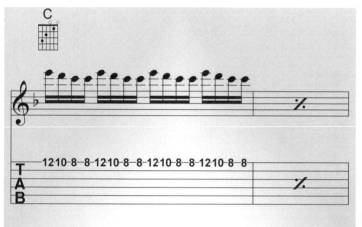

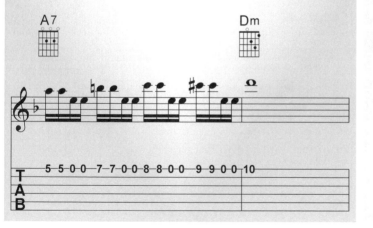

Example 02 Lead

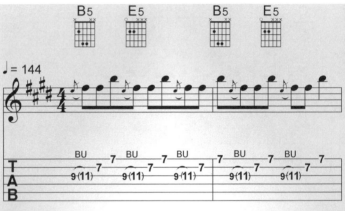

With distortion.
Drop all strings by 1 semitone.

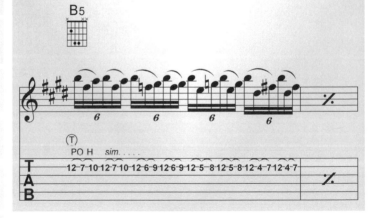

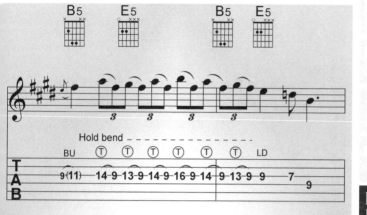

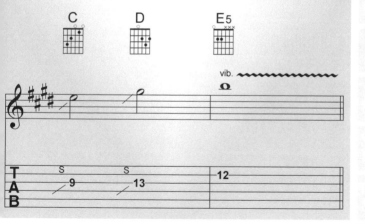

Hard Rock

Example 03 Lead

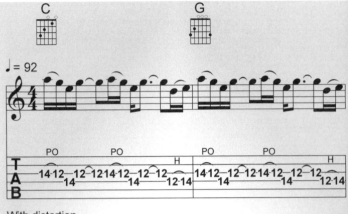

With distortion.

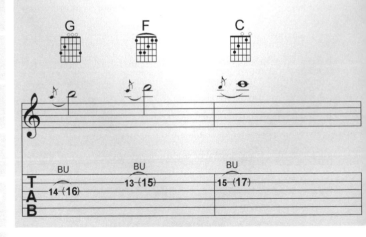

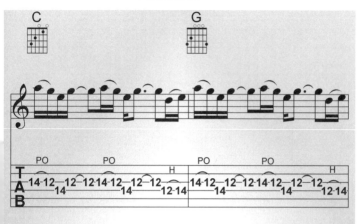

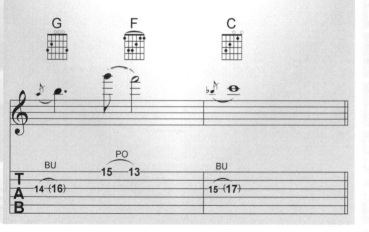

Example 04 Lead

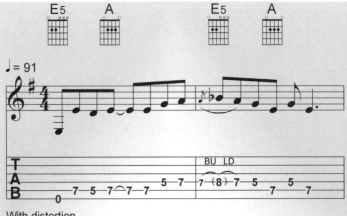

With distortion.

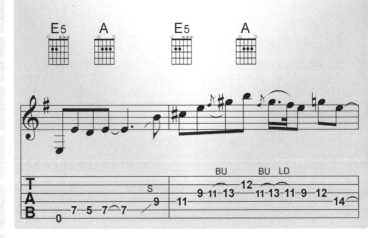

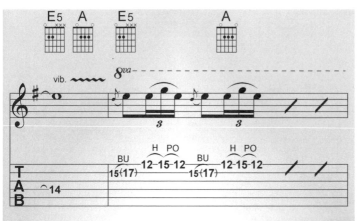

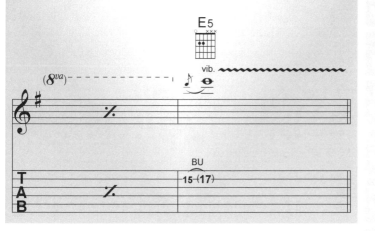

Example 05 Rhythm

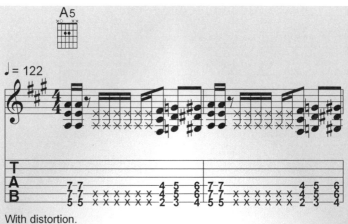

With distortion.
Drop all strings by 1 semitone.

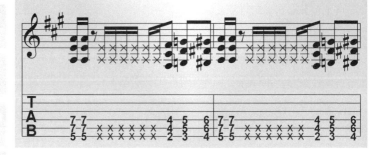

Example 06 Rhythm

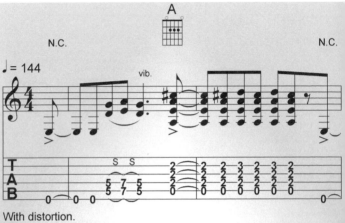

With distortion.
Drop all strings by 1 semitone.

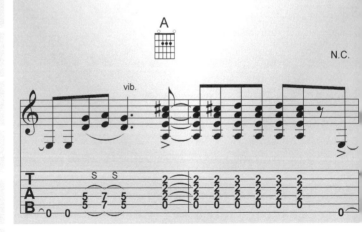

Hard Rock

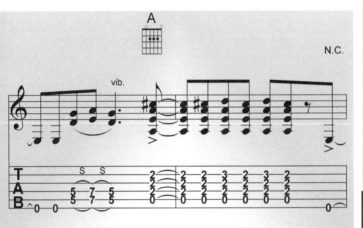

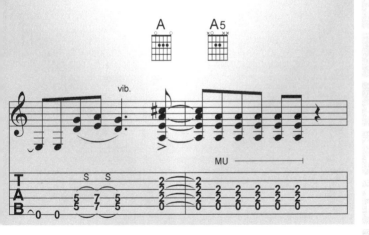

Example 07 Rhythm

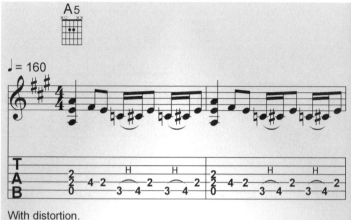

With distortion.

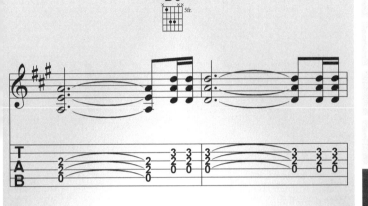

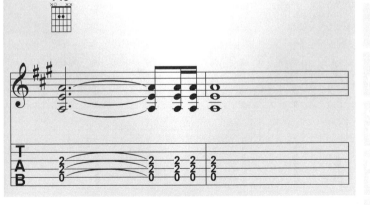

Example 08 Rhythm

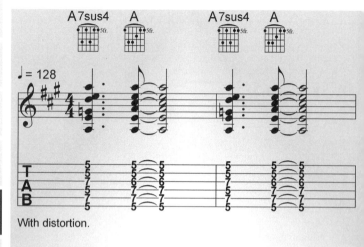

With distortion.

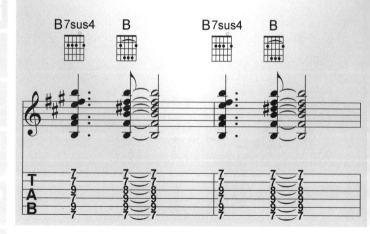

Hard Rock

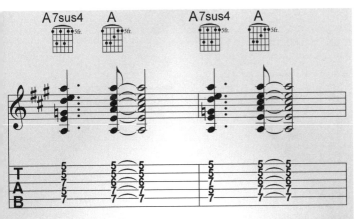

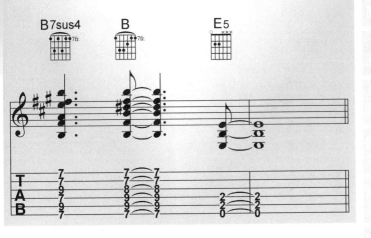

Example 09 Riff

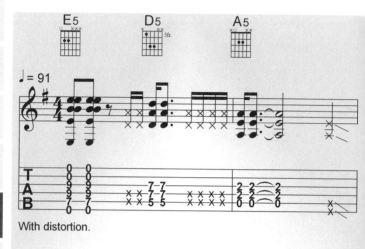

With distortion.

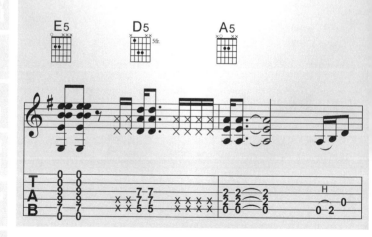

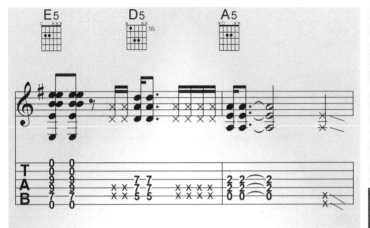

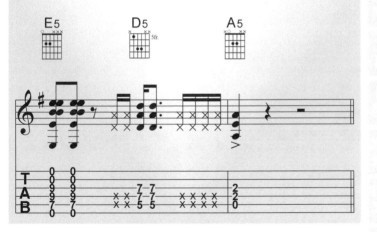

Example 10 Riff

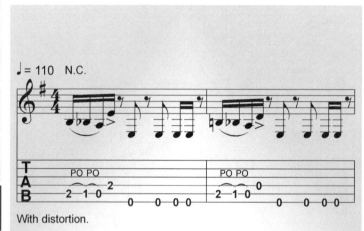

With distortion.

Example 11 Riff

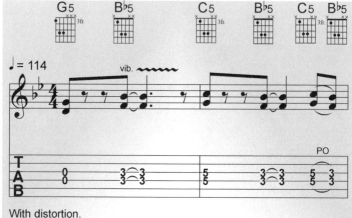

With distortion.

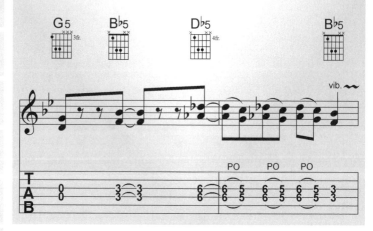

Hard Rock

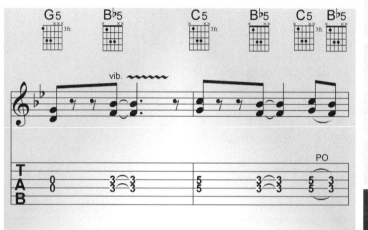

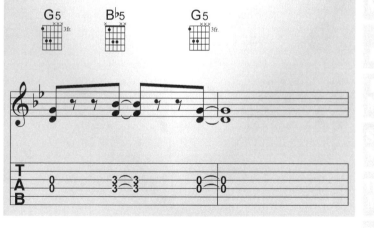

Example 12 Riff

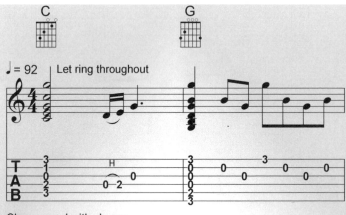

Clean sound with chorus.
Drop all strings by 1 semitone.

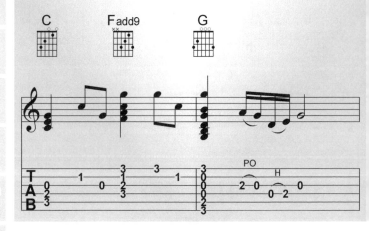

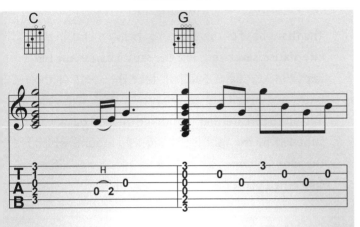

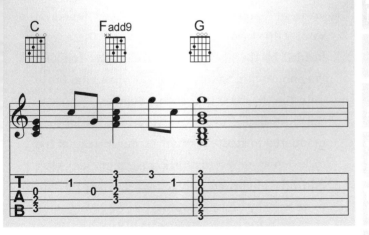

Heavy Metal

The first phase of the growth of heavy metal, in the late Sixties, saw bands like the Yardbirds, Cream, Led Zeppelin and Black Sabbath take the roots of the blues and amplify it to produce a loud, distorted and often threatening sound. The musical basis was supplied by the guitar playing riffs around which the songs were built, while the lyrics often concerned black magic and the occult.

The biggest heavy bands like Zeppelin, Judas Priest and Sabbath became stadium-fillers, and a new wave of bands grew up that played low-level venues (the New Wave of Heavy Metal). These were headed by the likes of Iron Maiden, Def Leppard, Praying Mantis, Saxon and Angelwitch who broke onto the UK scene in the early Eighties. Of course, the most successful of these 'grass roots' bands then graduated to stadia themselves, but instead of the cycle being repeated musicians splintered away into less publicized sub-genres, diversifying into more lyrically explicit material.

Heavy
Metal

Example 01 Lead

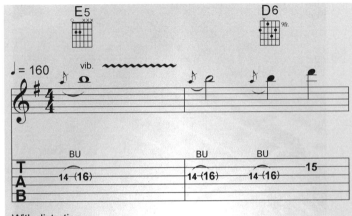

With distortion.

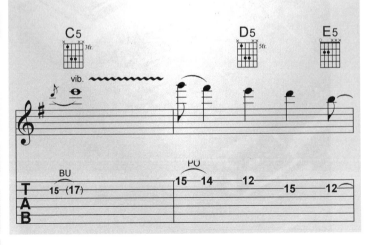

Heavy Metal

Black Metal

Death Metal

Doom Metal

Goth Rock

Grind Core

Hard Rock

Heavy Metal

Nu Rock

Prog Metal

Speed Metal

Thrash Metal

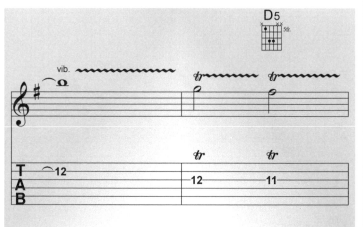

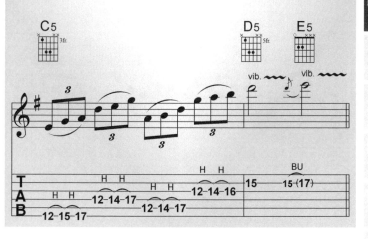

Example 02 Lead

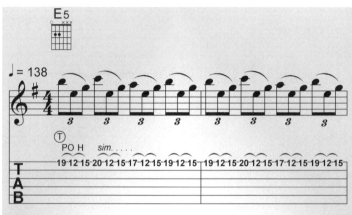

With distortion.

Heavy
Metal

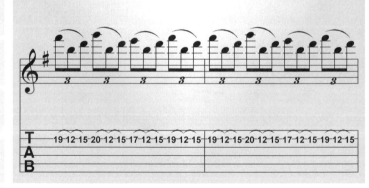

Heavy Metal

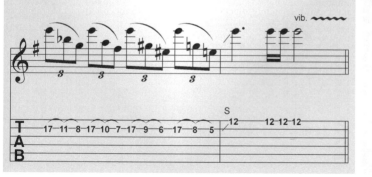

Example 03 Lead

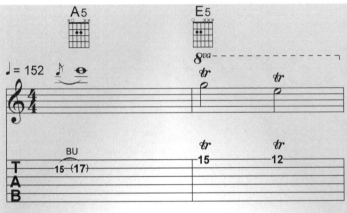

With distortion.

Heavy Metal

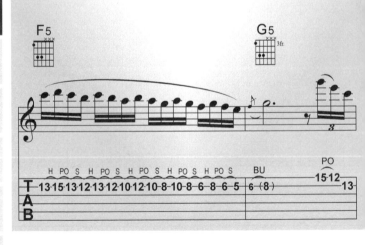

Heavy Metal

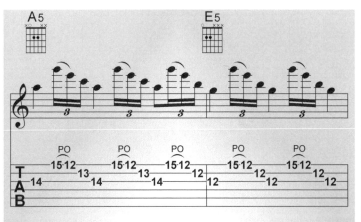

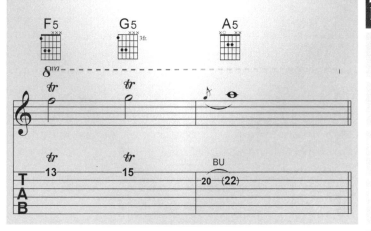

Example 04 Lead

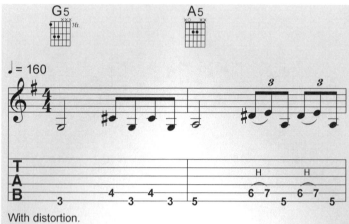

With distortion.

Heavy
Metal

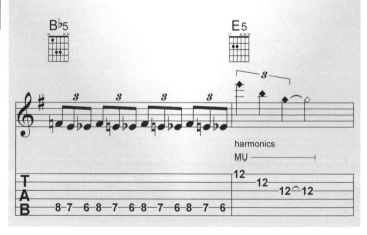

harmonics
MU

Heavy Metal

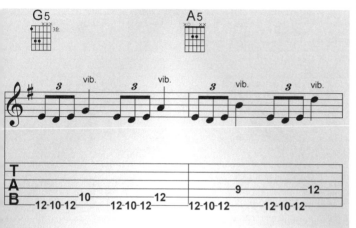

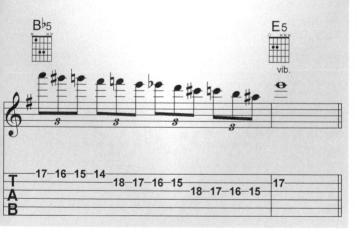

Example 05 Rhythm

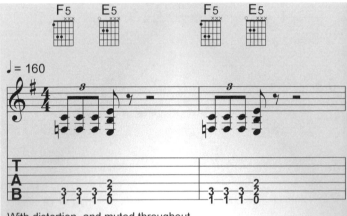

With distortion, and muted throughout.

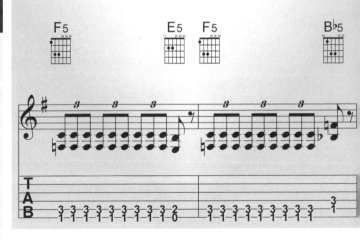

Heavy Metal

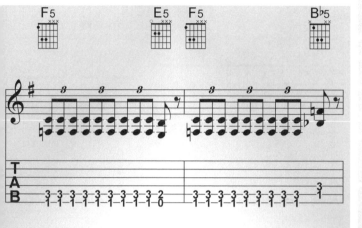

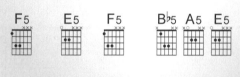

Heavy
Metal

Example 06 Rhythm

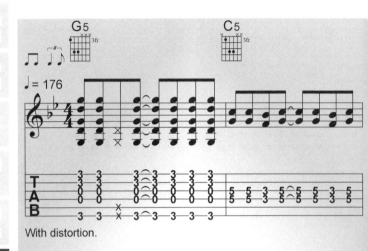

With distortion.

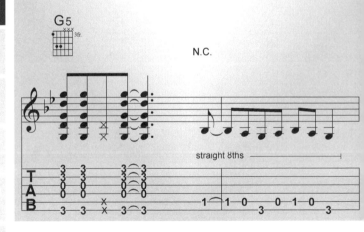

Heavy Metal

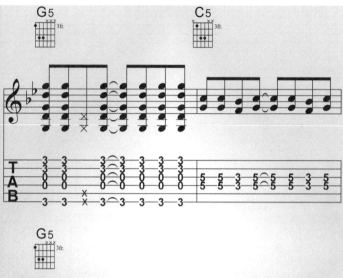

Example 07 Rhythm

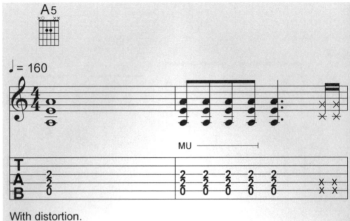

With distortion.

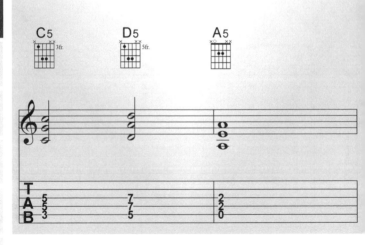

Heavy Metal

A5

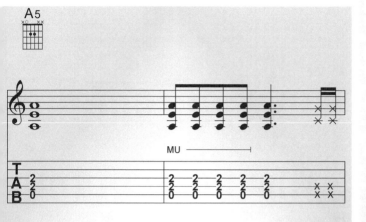

MU |————————————|

C5 3fr. **D5** 5fr. **E5**

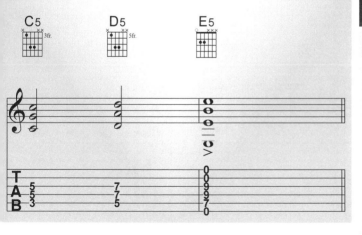

Example 08 Rhythm

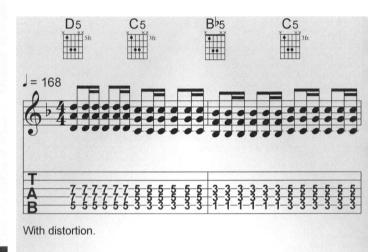

With distortion.

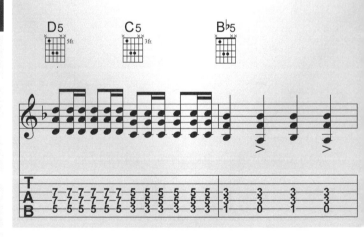

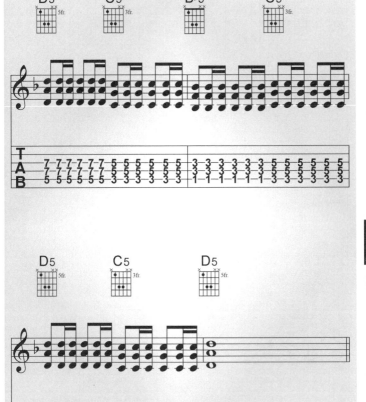

Example 09 Riff

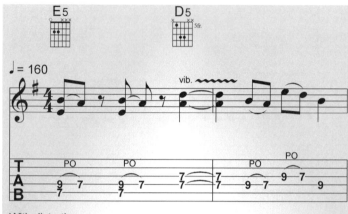

With distortion.

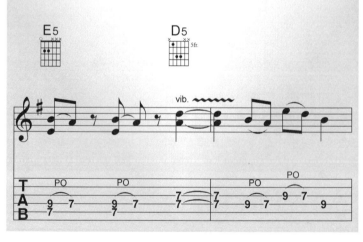

Heavy Metal

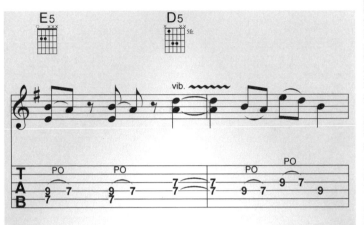

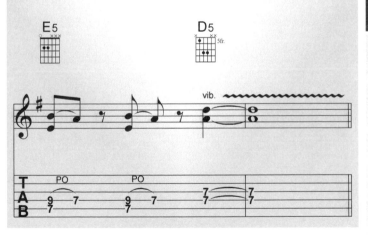

Example 10 Riff

With distortion.

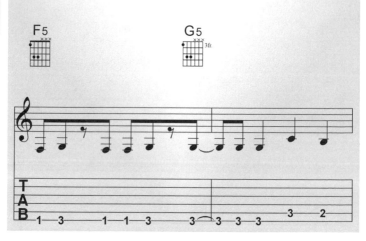

Heavy Metal

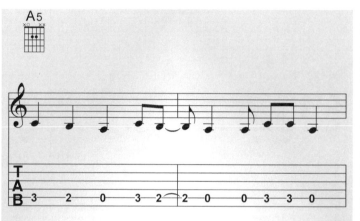

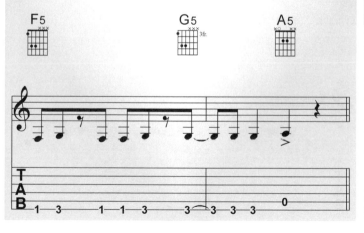

Example 11 Riff

Clean sound with chorus.

Heavy Metal

Example 12 Riff

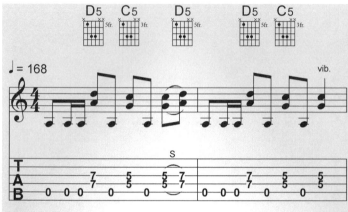

With distortion.

Heavy Metal

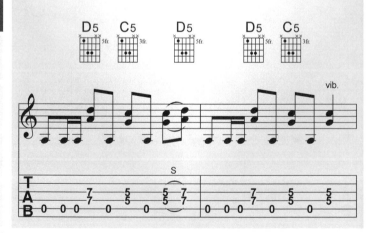

Heavy Metal

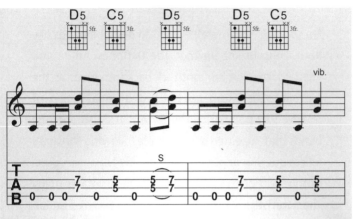

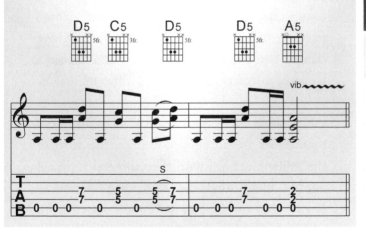

Nu Rock

Nu rock (also nu metal) is used to describe bands like Korn, Limp Bizkit, Slipknot, the Deftones, Amen and Papa Roach, who brought rock back into focus as the current millennium approached after a period of relative low popularity. The term is used to describe bands that appeared in the decade following Nirvana's all-conquering popularity in the early Nineties – post-grunge is another label. The music incorporates many characteristics of grunge, notably the distorted guitar, angst-filled lyrics and loud-chorus-quiet-verse dynamic, but reproduces it in a radio-friendly, commercial way. This has ensured the genre's mainstream popularity, but many grunge fans have claimed that this is a sellout. There has also been a tendency to incorporate MCs or DJs within the line-up.

While some of its protagonists have distanced themselves from the genre since the turn of the millennium – 'I hate the nu-metal term... it doesn't mean anything' said Korn's Jonathan Davis – they continue to make their presence felt with various projects.

Example 01 Lead

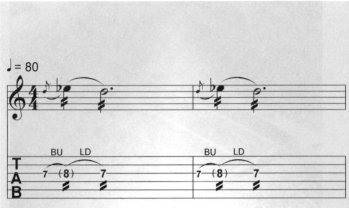

With echo and distortion.

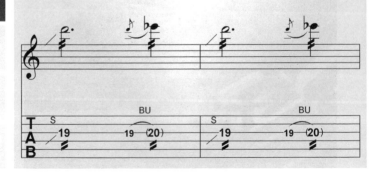

Nu Rock

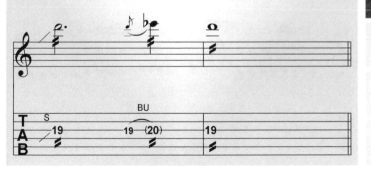

Nu Rock

Example 02 Lead

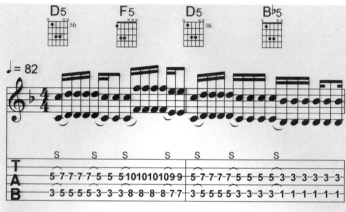

With distortion.

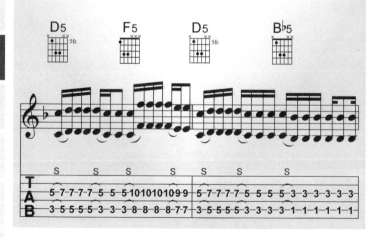

Nu Rock

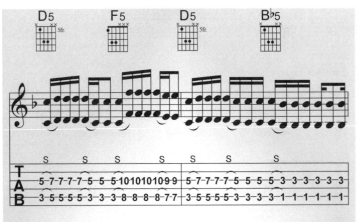

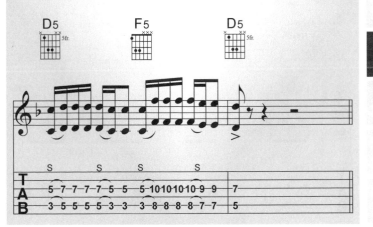

Example 03 Lead

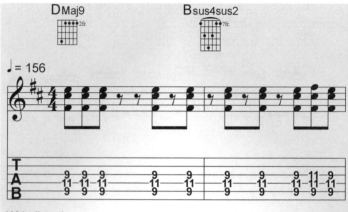

With distortion.

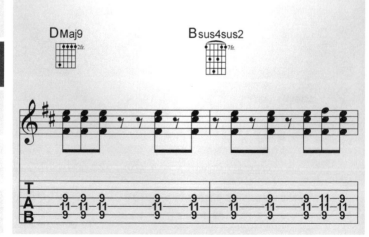

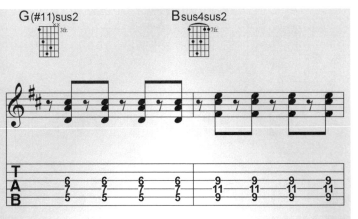

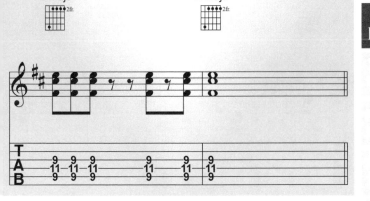

Example 04 Rhythm

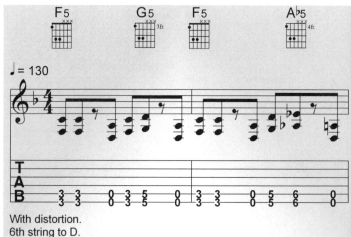

With distortion.
6th string to D.

Nu
Rock

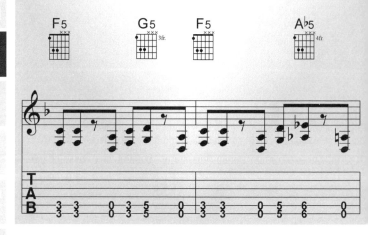

Nu Rock

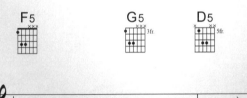

Example 05 Rhythm

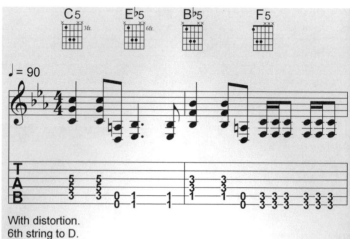

With distortion.
6th string to D.

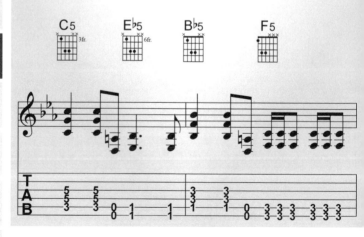

Example 06 Rhythm

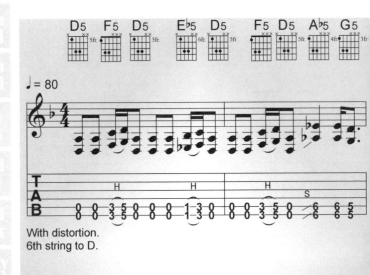

With distortion.
6th string to D.

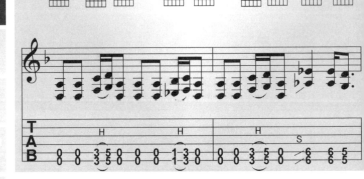

Nu Rock

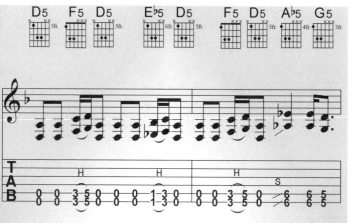

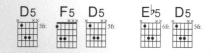

Example 07 Rhythm

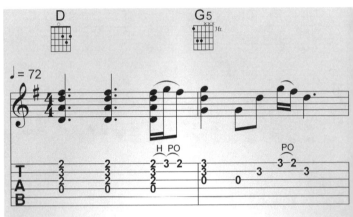

With clean sound.

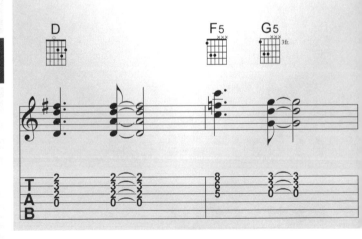

Nu Rock

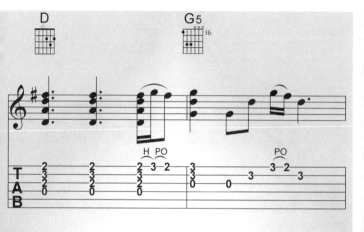

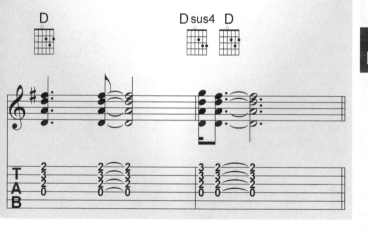

Example 08 Rhythm

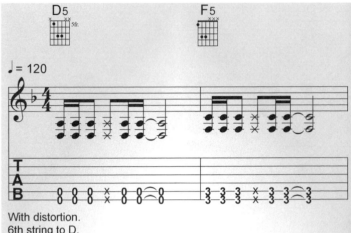

With distortion.
6th string to D.

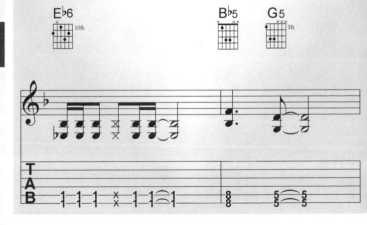

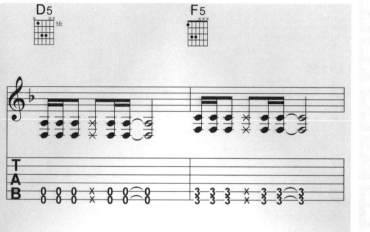

Example 09 Riff

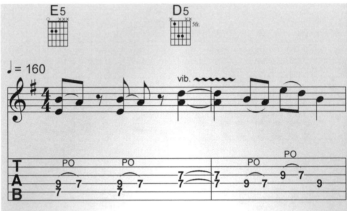

With distortion.

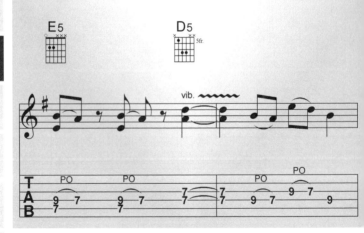

Nu Rock

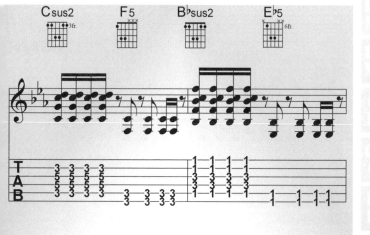

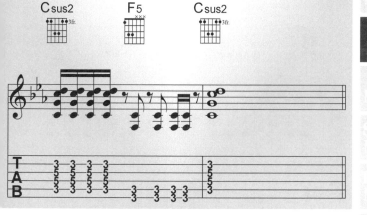

Black Metal

Death Metal

Doom Metal

Goth

Grunge / Classic

Hard Rock

Heavy Metal

Nu Rock

Prog Metal

Speed Metal

Indie / Alternative

Example 10 Riff

With distortion.
6th string to D.

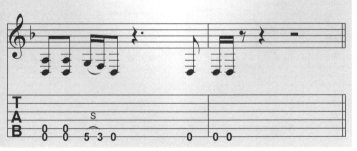

Black Metal

Death Metal

Doom Metal

Goth Rock

Grind Core

Hard Rock

Heavy Metal

Nu Rock

Prog Metal

Speed Metal

Thrash Metal

Example 11 Riff

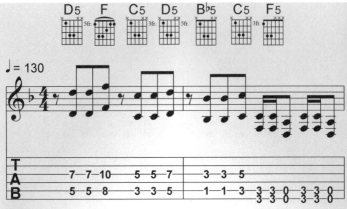

With distortion.
6th string to D.

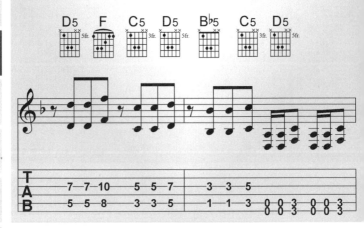

Nu Rock

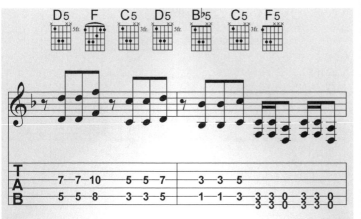

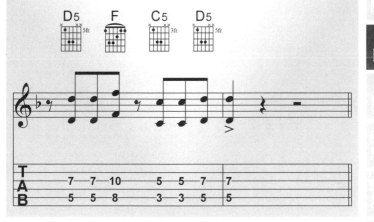

Black
Metal

Death
Metal

Doom
Metal

Goth
Rock

Grind
Core

Hard
Rock

Heavy
Metal

Nu
Rock

Prog
Metal

Speed
Metal

Thrash
Metal

Virtuo
Metal

Example 12 Riff

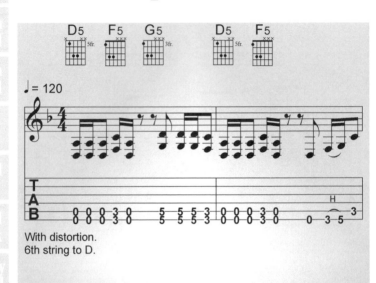

With distortion.
6th string to D.

Nu Rock

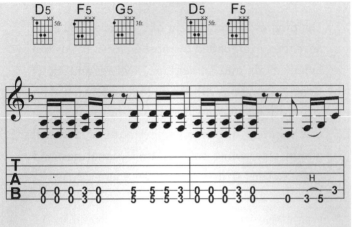

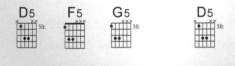

Black Metal

Death Metal

Doom Metal

Goth Rock

Grind Core

Hard Rock

Heavy Metal

Nu Rock

Prog Metal

Speed Metal

Thrash Metal

Virtue Metal

Prog Metal

The progressive movement of the Sixties and early Seventies, exemplified by mostly British bands like Emerson Lake and Palmer, Pink Floyd, Yes and (early) Genesis, came up with music that largely relied on virtuosity for its appeal. Complex music that was often spread out across the length of a (vinyl) album side, while shifting time signatures and complex song structures were de rigueur.

Progressive rock suddenly fell out of favour in the mid Seventies with the advent of punk and more direct forms of music, but would enjoy a Nineties revival which saw mostly American bands like Dream Theater, Spock's Beard and Transatlantic merge the complexities of the prog genre with a harder-hitting, guitar-led edge.

Prog metal bands tackle their complex rhythms and song structures with traditional rock instrumentation, unlike avant-garde metal which uses unusual sounds and instruments. Current exponents include Pain of Salvation, Opeth, Ayreon, King's X and Rush.

Prog
Metal

Example 01 Lead

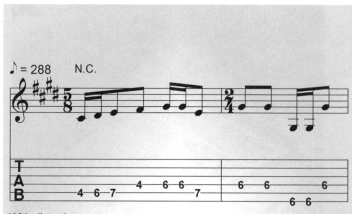

With distortion.

Example 02 Lead

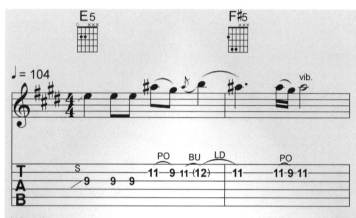

With distortion.

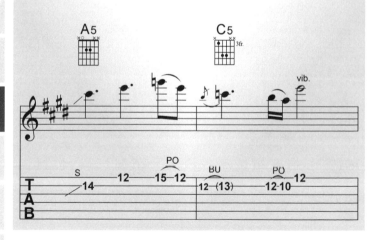

Prog Metal

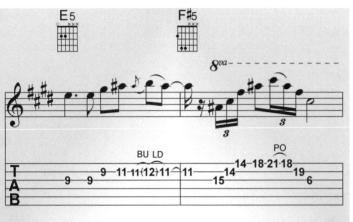

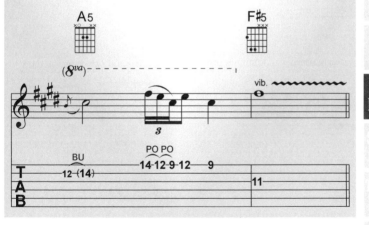

Blues Metal

Death Metal

Doom Metal

Goth Rock

Grind Core

Hard Rock

Heavy Metal

Nu Rock

Prog Metal

Speed Metal

Thrash Metal

Viking Metal

Example 03 Lead

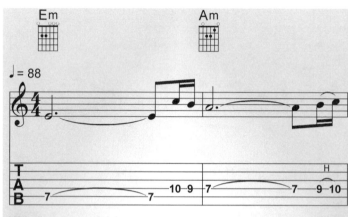

With distortion and delay.
Drop all strings by 1 semitone.

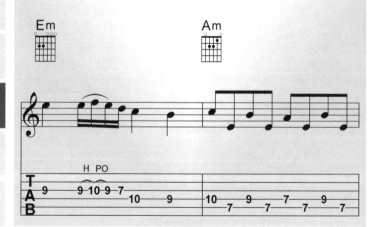

Prog Metal

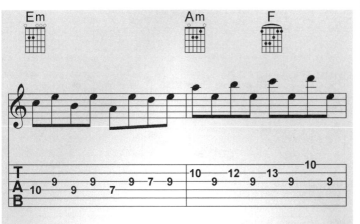

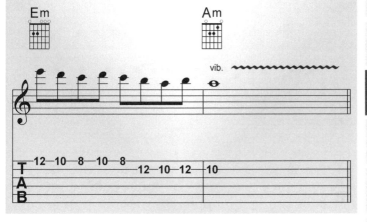

Example 04 Lead

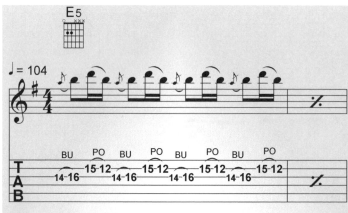

With distortion and delay.
Drop all strings by 1 semitone.

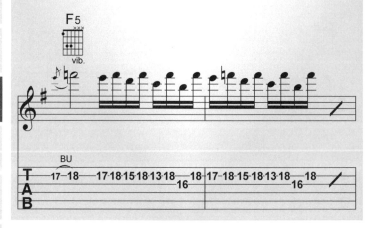

Prog Metal

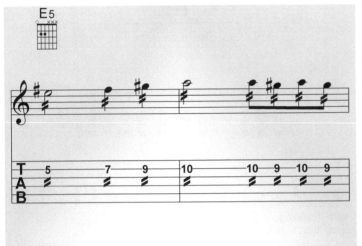

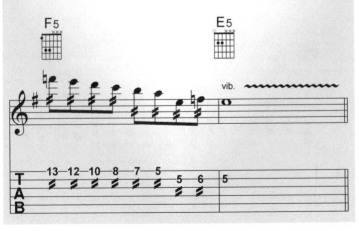

Black Metal

Death Metal

Doom Metal

Goth Rock

Grind Core

Hard Rock

Heavy Metal

Nu Rock

Prog Metal

Speed Metal

Thrash Metal

Virtue Metal

Example 05 Rhythm

With distortion.
Drop all strings by 1 semitone.

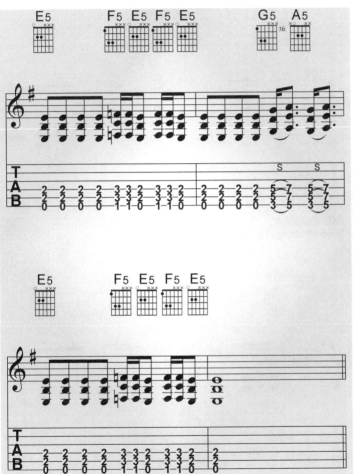

Example 06 Rhythm

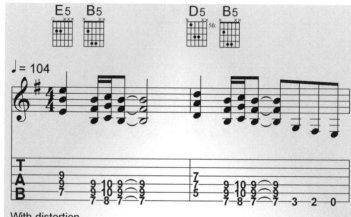

With distortion.
Drop all strings by 1 semitone.

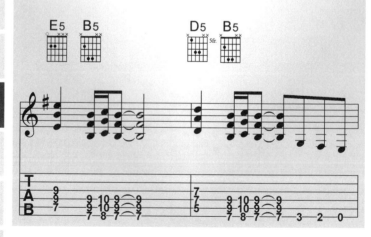

Prog Metal

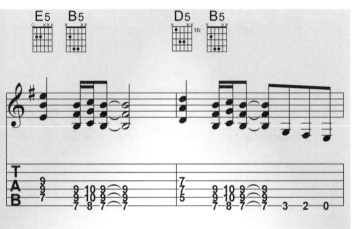

Example 07 Rhythm

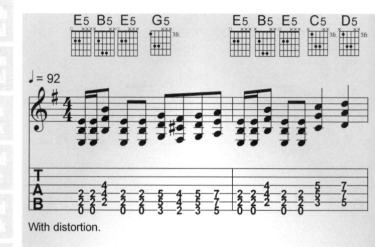

With distortion.

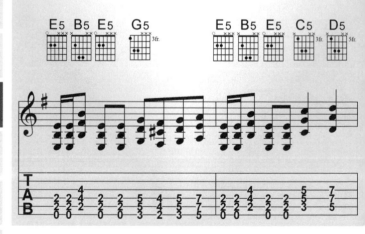

Prog Metal

Black Metal

Death Metal

Doom Metal

Goth Rock

Grind Core

Hard Rock

Heavy Metal

Nu Rock

Prog Metal

Speed Metal

Thrash Metal

Viking Metal

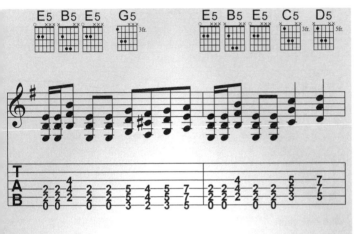

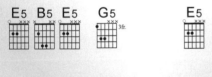

279

Example 08 Rhythm

With distortion.
Drop all strings by 1 semitone.

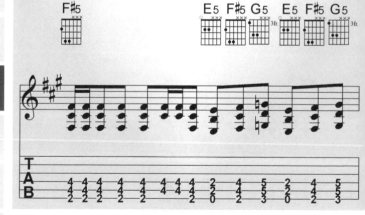

Prog Metal

Prog Metal

Example 09 Riff

Black
Metal

Death
Metal

Doom
Metal

Goth
Rock

Grind
Core

Hard
Rock

Heavy
Metal

Nu
Rock

Prog
Metal

Speed
Metal

Thrash
Metal

Virtuo
Metal

Let ring.
Drop all strings by 1 semitone.

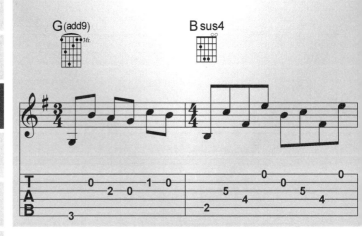

Prog Metal

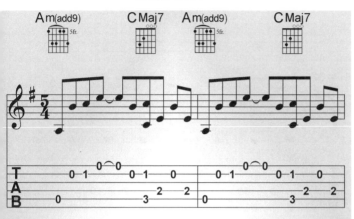

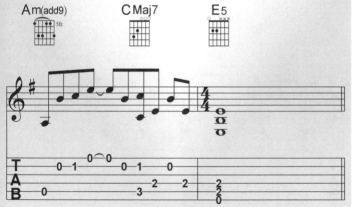

Black Metal

Death Metal

Doom Metal

Goth Rock

Grind Core

Hard Rock

Heavy Metal

Nu Rock

Prog Metal

Speed Metal

Thrash Metal

Virtuo Metal

Example 10 Riff

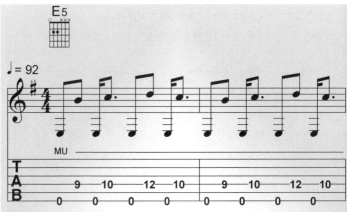

With distortion.
Drop all strings by 1 semitone.

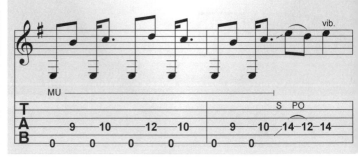

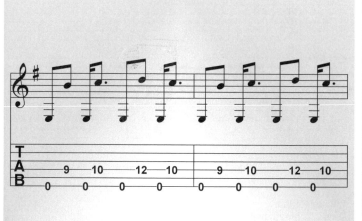

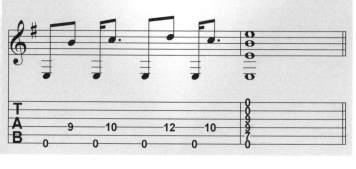

Example 11 Riff

With distortion.
Drop all strings by 1 semitone.

Prog Metal

Prog Metal

Example 12 Riff

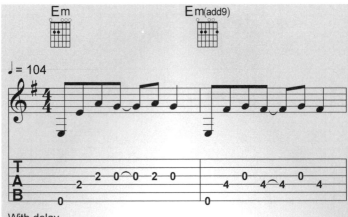

With delay.
Let ring throughout.

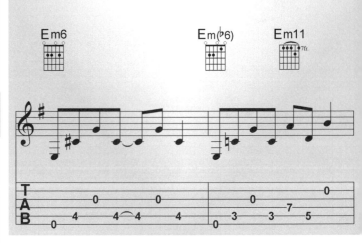

Prog Metal

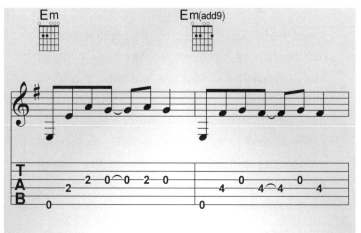

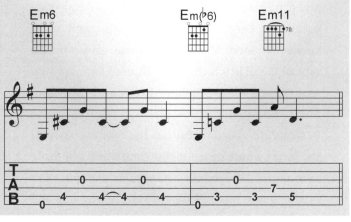

Black Metal

Death Metal

Doom Metal

Goth Rock

Grind Core

Hard Rock

Heavy Metal

Nu Rock

Prog Metal

Speed Metal

Thrash Metal

Virtuo Metal

Speed Metal

Speed metal was created in the Eighties from a combination of hardcore and the New Wave of British Heavy Metal. To quote one critic, the effect was 'suffocating, immobilizing, neurotic and paranoid'. Motörhead were one of speed metal's earliest and most commercially successful proponents, but there were bands like Slayer, Anthrax, Overkill and Megadeth whose early output could be classed as speed metal.

Lyrical topics like war, pollution, nuclear weapons and corporate domination were imparted by a male vocalist in deep tones, or sometimes even semi-spoken/shouted. Musically, this was an up-tempo type of metal in which guitarists used palm muting as a strumming technique to produce bursts of alternating rhythms. Complex and often inventive in structure, speed metal was the musical basis for the forthcoming death metal, thrash and grindcore sub-genres. It remains particularly popular in Japan, where modern bands like Gamma Ray and Primal Fear find a ready audience.

Example 01 Lead

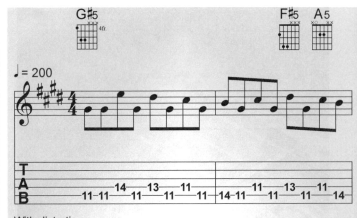

With distortion.

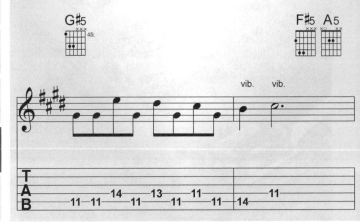

Speed Metal

Black Metal

Death Metal

Doom Metal

Goth Rock

Grind Core

Hard Rock

Heavy Metal

Nu Rock

Prog Metal

Speed Metal

Thrash Metal

Viking Metal

Example 02 Lead

With distortion.

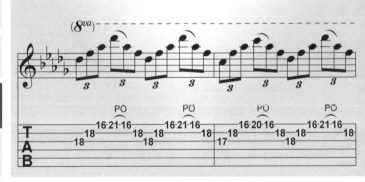

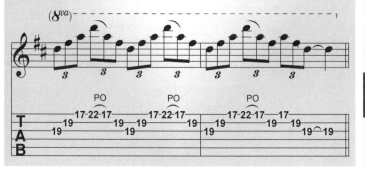

Speed Metal

Example 03 Lead

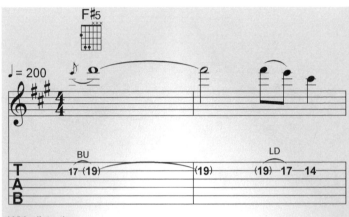

With distortion.

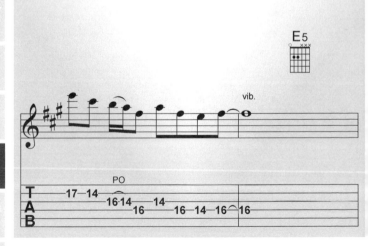

F#5

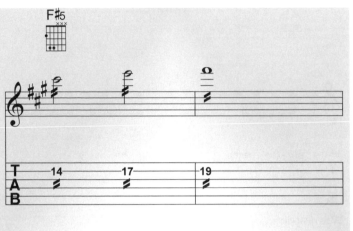

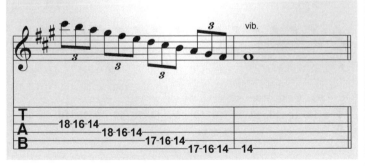

Example 04 Lead

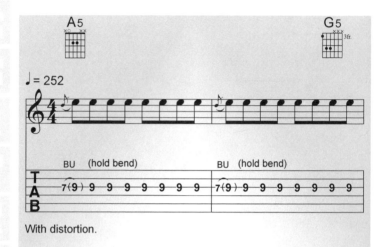

With distortion.

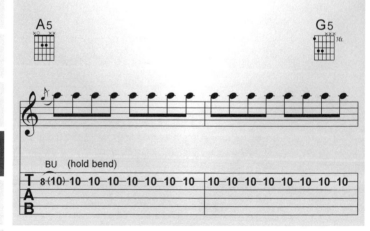

Speed Metal

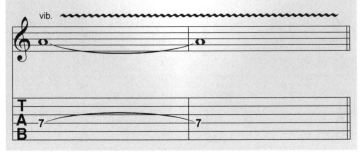

Example 05 Rhythm

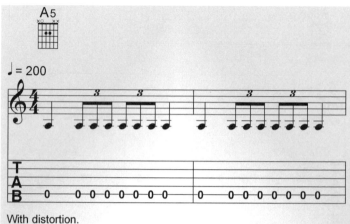

With distortion.

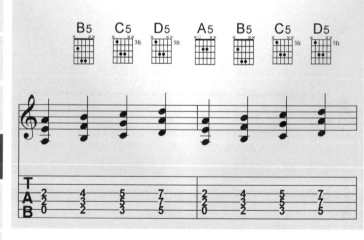

Speed Metal

Black
Metal

Death
Metal

Doom
Metal

Goth
Rock

Grind
Core

Hard
Rock

Heavy
Metal

Nu
Rock

Prog
Metal

**Speed
Metal**

Thrash
Metal

Virtuo
Metal

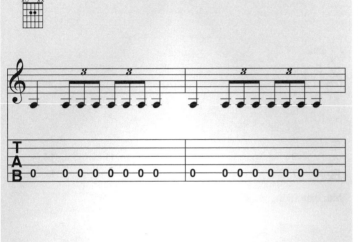

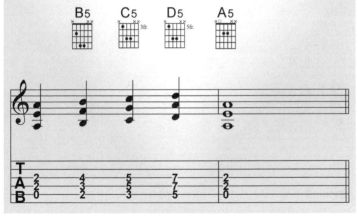

Example 06 Rhythm

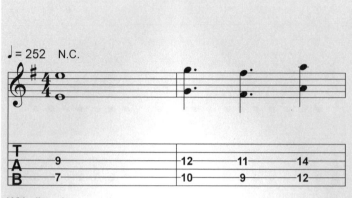

With distortion.

Speed Metal

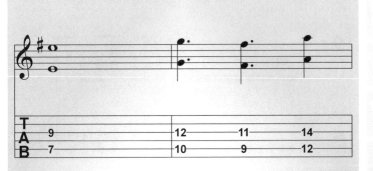

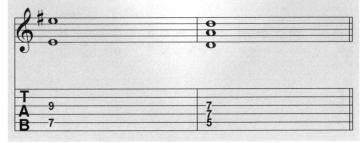

Speed
Metal

Example 07 Rhythm

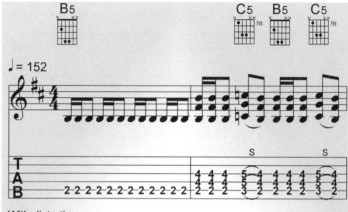

With distortion.

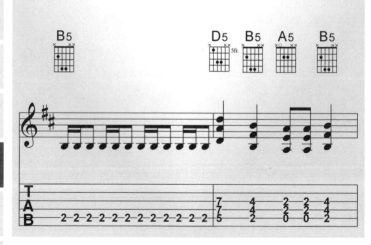

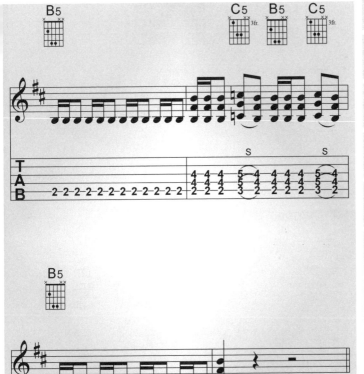

Black
Metal

Death
Metal

Doom
Metal

Goth
Rock

Grind
Core

Hard
Rock

Heavy
Metal

Nu
Rock

Prog
Metal

Speed
Metal

Thrash
Metal

Virtuo
Metal

Example 08 Rhythm

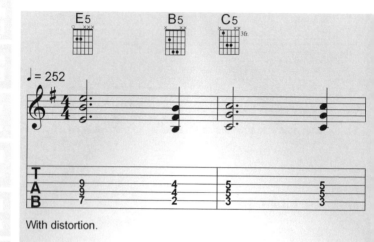

With distortion.

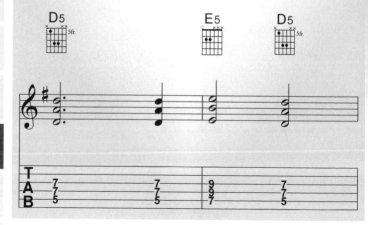

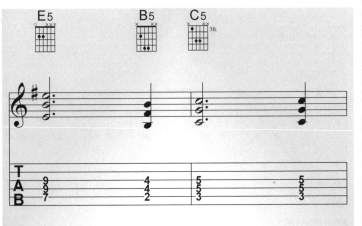

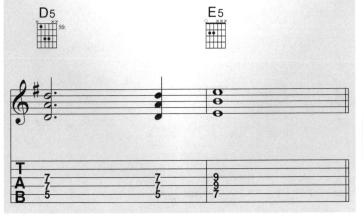

Example 09 Riff

Black
Metal

Death
Metal

Doom
Metal

Goth
Rock

Grind
Core

Hard
Rock

Heavy
Metal

Nu
Rock

Prog
Metal

**Speed
Metal**

Thrash
Metal

Virtuo
Metal

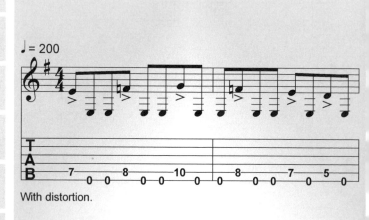

With distortion.

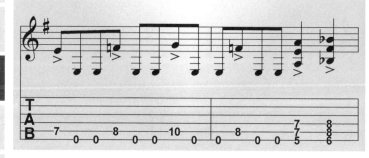

Speed Metal

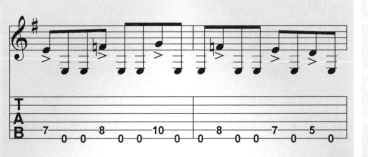

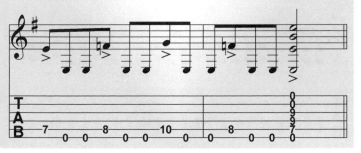

Example 10 Riff

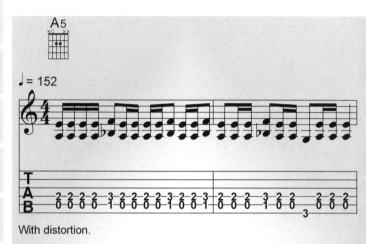

With distortion.

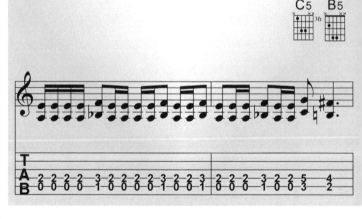

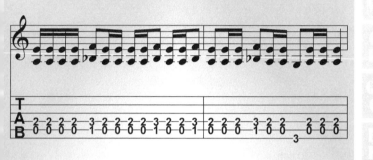

Black Metal

Death Metal

Doom Metal

Indie Rock

Grind Core

Hard Rock

Heavy Metal

Nu Rock

Prog Metal

Speed Metal

Thrash Metal

Metal

Example 11 Riff

With distortion.

Black
Metal

Death
Metal

Doom
Metal

Goth
Rock

Grind
Core

Hard
Rock

Heavy
Metal

Nu
Rock

Prog
Metal

Speed
Metal

Thrash
Metal

Virtuo
Metal

Speed Metal

Example 12 Riff

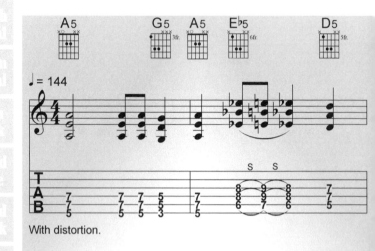

With distortion.

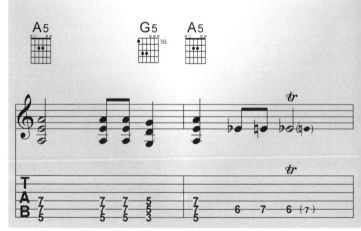

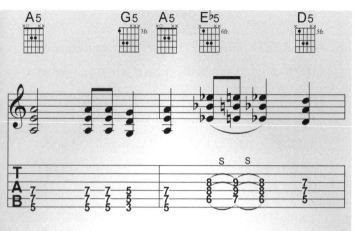

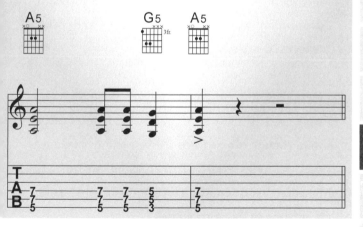

Black Metal

Death Metal

Doom Metal

Goth Rock

Grind Core

Hard Rock

Heavy Metal

Nu Rock

Prog Metal

Speed Metal

Thrash Metal

Virtuo Metal

Thrash Metal

With a title reflecting the fact that guitars were attacked or 'thrashed', thrash emerged when hardcore and metal collided, combining a punk attitude with metal riffs and lyrical topics. Songs could be as short as under a minute with just one or two riffs behind a central lyrical idea, often political and/or nihilistic in nature, expressed in verse and chorus form. Guitar riffs were pitched low, solos high and vocals shouted at high speed. While musicianship was often not of a high standard, drumming was particularly frantic and often featured double bass drums.

Metallica's *Kill 'Em All* and Slayer's *Show No Mercy* were said to define the genre when released in 1983, though others trace the beginnings of thrash back to Judas Priest. German band Kreator and Brazilian band Sepultura were among noted bands to emerge in the mid Eighties.

Black
Metal

Death
Metal

Doom
Metal

Goth
Rock

Grind
Core

Hard
Rock

Heavy
Metal

Nu
Rock

Prog
Metal

Speed
Metal

Thrash
Metal

Virtuo
Metal

Black
Metal

Death
Metal

Doom
Metal

Goth
Rock

Grind
Core

Hard
Rock

Heavy
Metal

Nu
Rock

Prog
Metal

Speed
Metal

**Thrash
Metal**

Virtue
Metal

Example 01 Lead

With distortion.

Thrash Metal

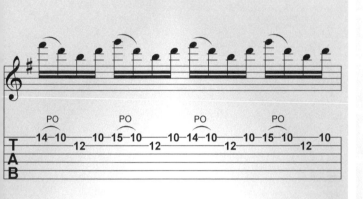

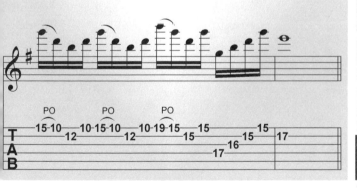

Example 02 Lead

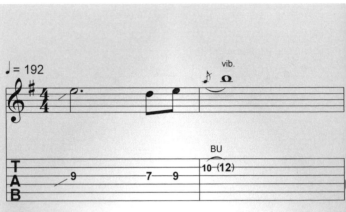

With distortion.

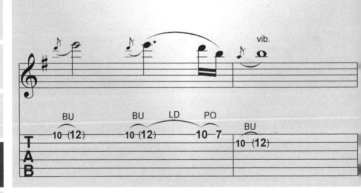

Thrash Metal

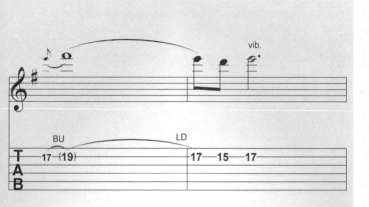

Thrash Metal

321

Example 03 Lead

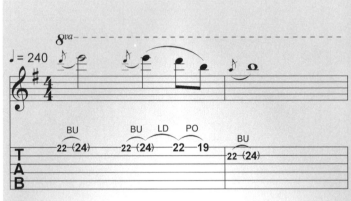

With distortion.
Drop all strings by 1 semitone.

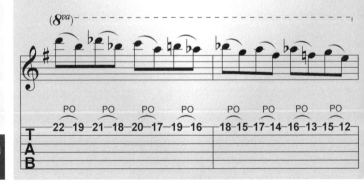

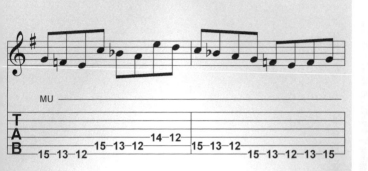

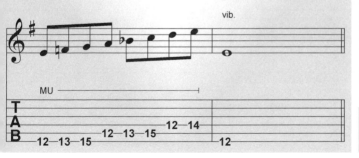

Example 04 Lead

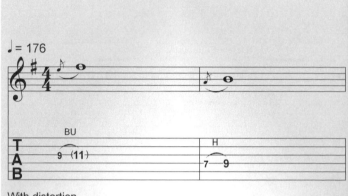

With distortion.

Thrash
Metal

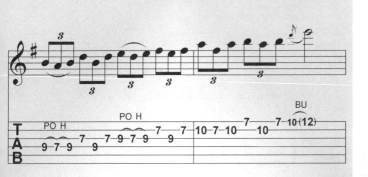

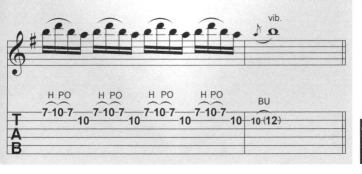

Example 05 Rhythm

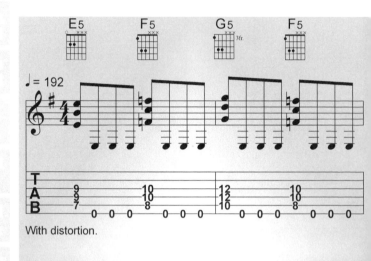

With distortion.

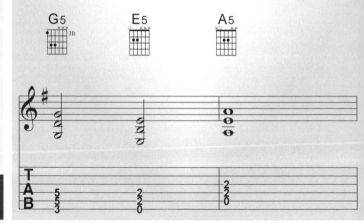

Thrash Metal

Thrash Metal

Example 06 Rhythm

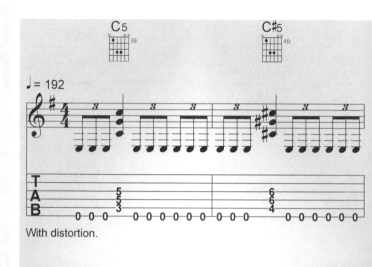

With distortion.

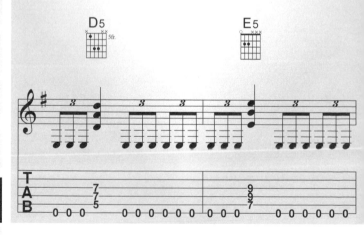

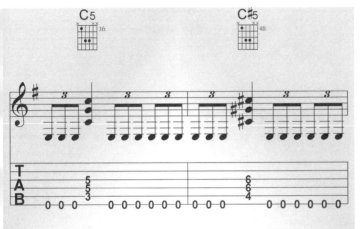

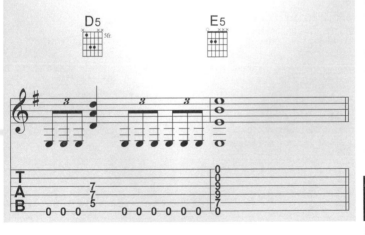

Example 07 Rhythm

With distortion.
Drop all strings by 1 semitone.

Thrash Metal

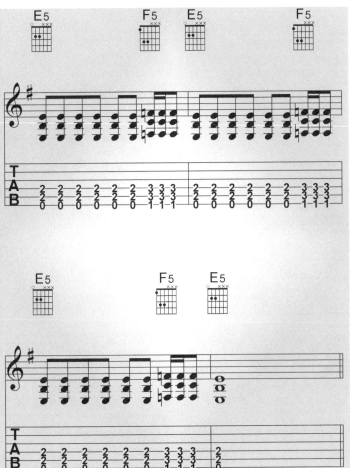

Thrash
Metal

Example 08 Rhythm

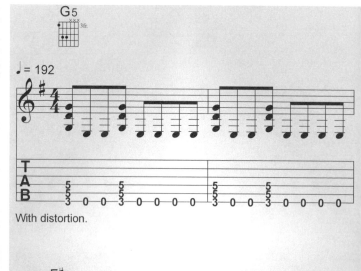

With distortion.

Thrash
Metal

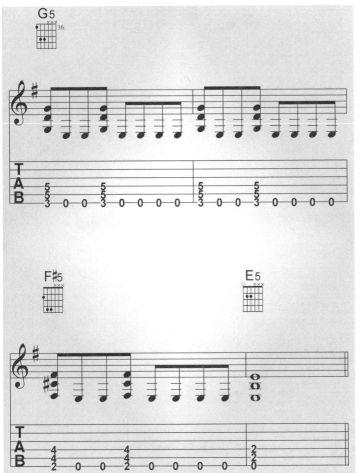

Thrash
Metal

Example 09 Riff

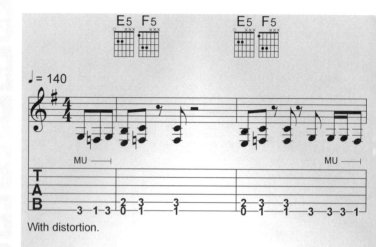

With distortion.

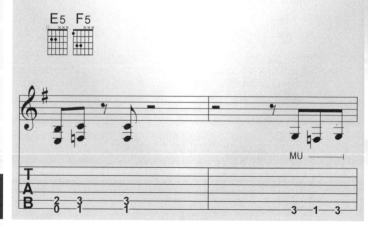

Thrash
Metal

Thrash Metal

Thrash
Metal

Example 10 Riff

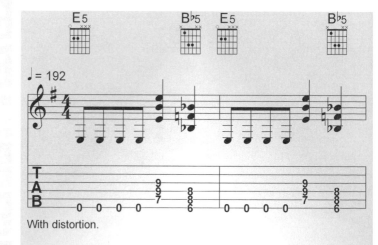

With distortion.

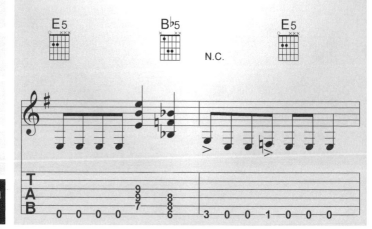

Thrash Metal

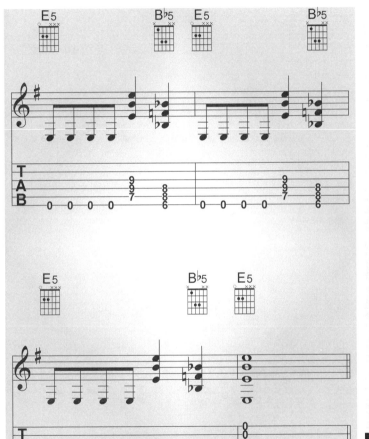

Example 11 Riff

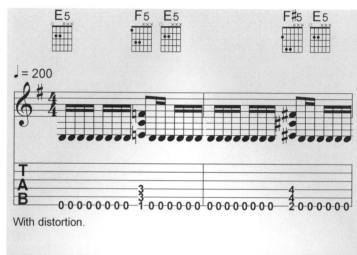

With distortion.

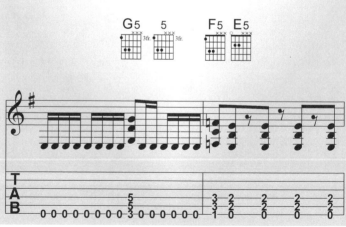

Thrash Metal

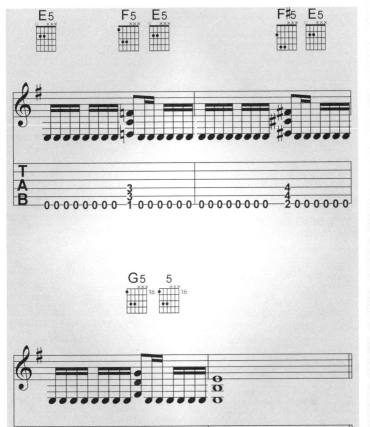

Example 12 Riff

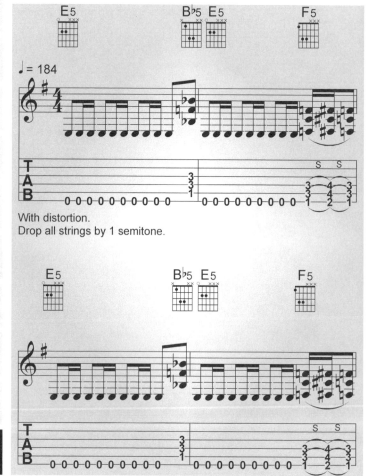

With distortion.
Drop all strings by 1 semitone.

Thrash Metal

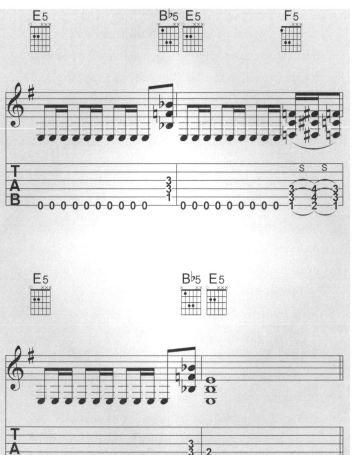

Virtuoso Metal

Virtuoso metal flew against punk's trend of image over technical skill. Eddie Van Halen paved the way for guitarists in the Eighties with his tapping and other tricks. Other virtuoso guitarists of note include Michael Angelo Batio, Vinnie Moore, Tony MacAlpine, Paul Gilbert (Racer X) and Jason Becker. The guitarists of virtuoso metal are all technically proficient (techniques used include tapping, sweep picking and fast alternate picking) and there is a large emphasis on speed. Virtuoso metal also includes the 'shredding' movement, said to have been inspired by attempts to imitate the Italian composer and violinist Niccolò Paganini.

A sub-genre, neoclassical metal, saw the likes of Swedish-born Yngwie Malmsteen integrate elements of classical music into metal and rock. He would transcribe and adapt classical music for the electric guitar, then introduce his modal progressions and classically-influenced techniques to the rock music of Alcatrazz and his own solo projects. A violin-like vibrato is one of his signature characteristics.

**Virtuo
Metal**

Example 01 Lead

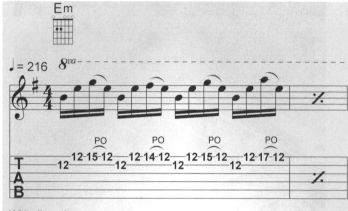

With distortion.
Drop all strings by 1 semitone.

Virtuo
Metal

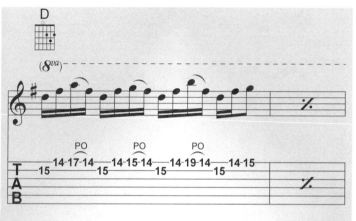

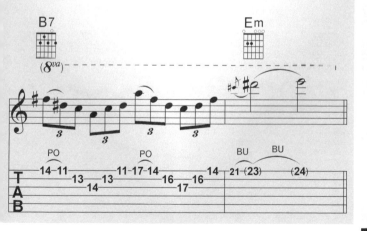

Example 02 Lead

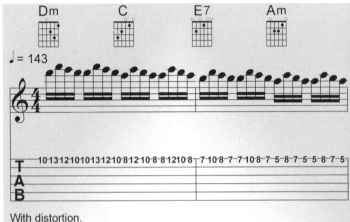

With distortion.
Drop all strings by 1 semitone.

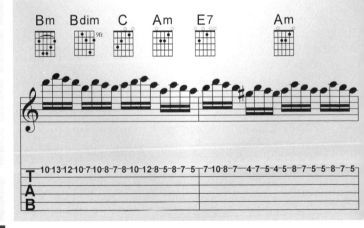

Virtuoso Metal

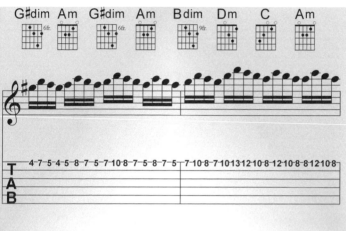

Example 03 Lead

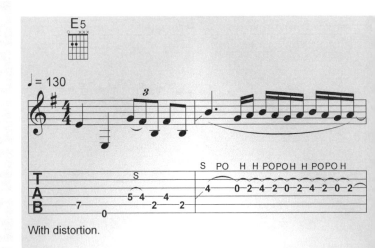

With distortion.

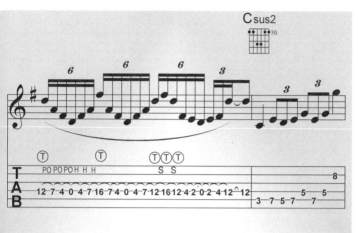

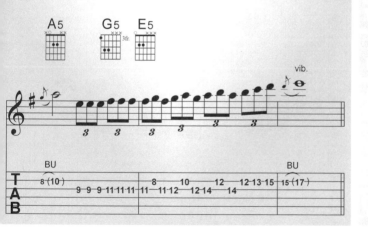

Example 04 Lead

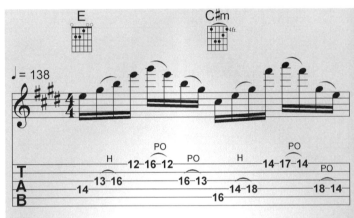

With distortion.

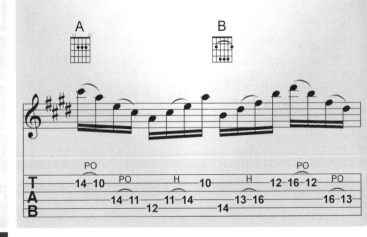

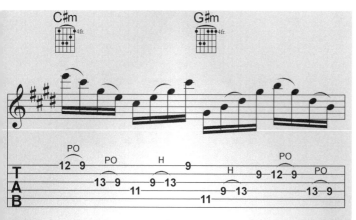

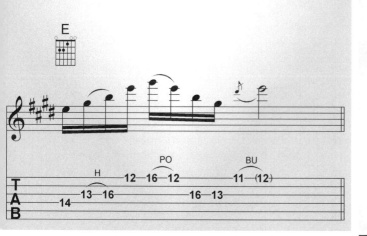

Example 05 Rhythm

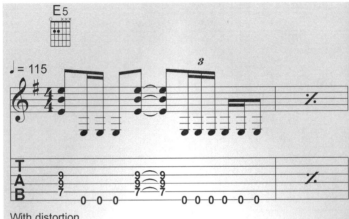

With distortion.

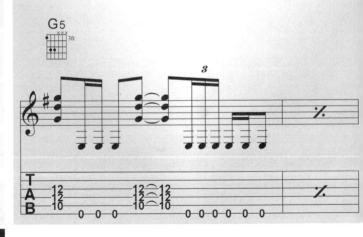

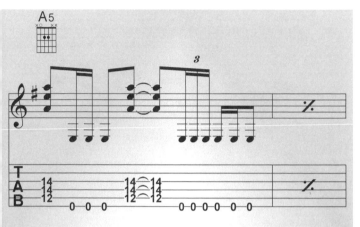

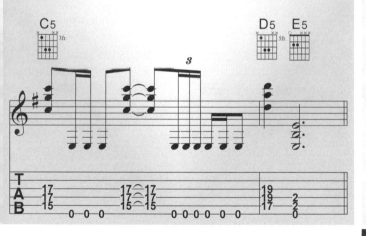

Example 06 Rhythm

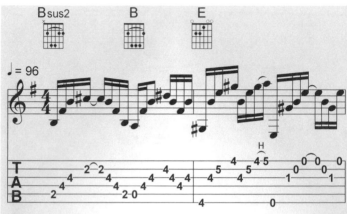

Let ring throughout.
Drop all strings by 1 semitone.

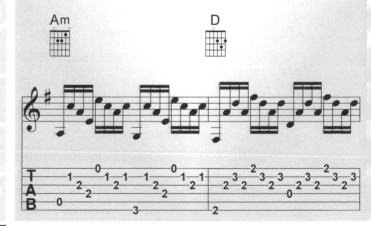

Virtuo
Metal

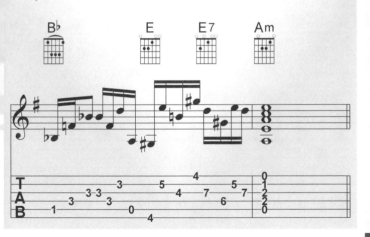

Example 07 Rhythm

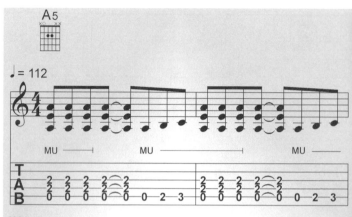

With distortion.
Drop all strings by 1 semitone.

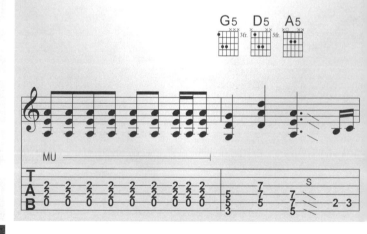

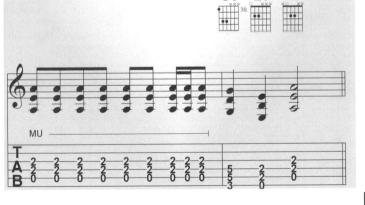

Example 08 Rhythm

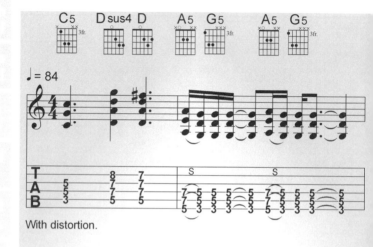

With distortion.

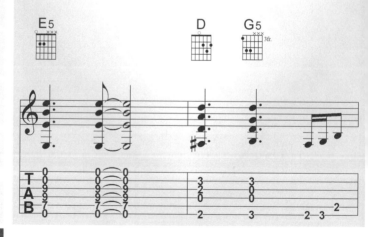

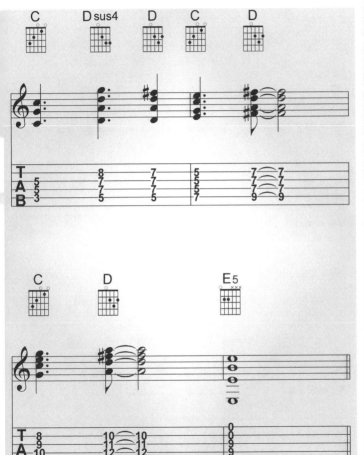

Example 09 Riff

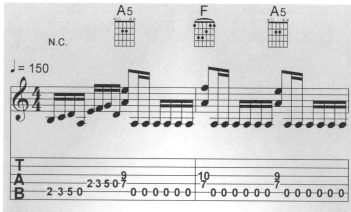

With distortion.
Drop all strings by 1 semitone.

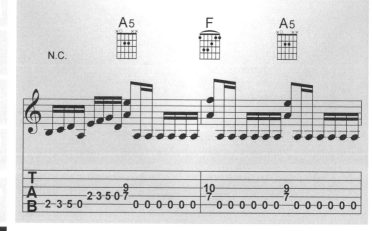

Virtuo Metal

Virtuoso Metal

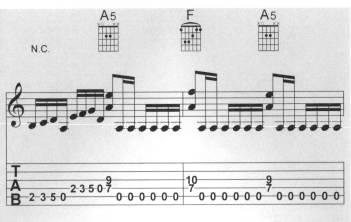

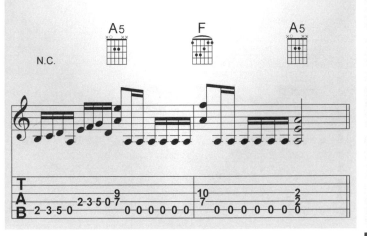

Example 10 Riff

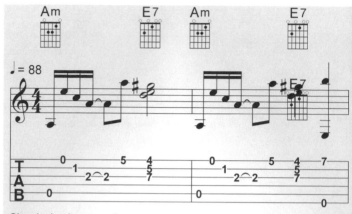

Classical guitar sound.
Drop all strings by 1 semitone.

Virtuoso Metal

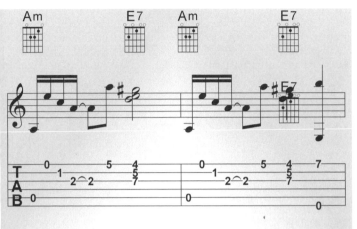

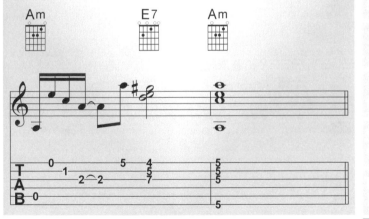

Virtuo
Metal

Example 11 Riff

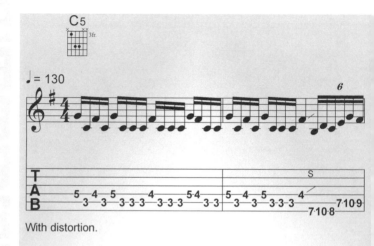

With distortion.

Virtuoso Metal

Example 12 Riff

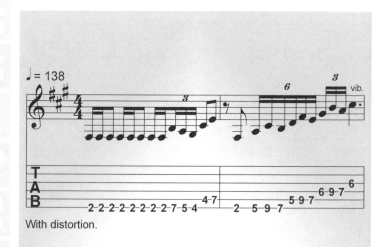

With distortion.

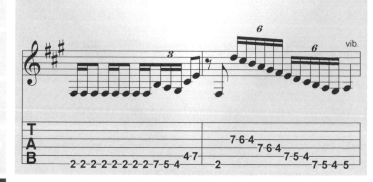

The History of Rock to Metal

Origins

The origins of rock come from the collision of blues and country that occurred in the Fifties in the music of a number of artists, most notably Elvis Presley.

The instrumentation of rock became based on the holy trinity of guitar, bass and drums. Gibson and Fender produced solid-bodied electric guitars such as the Les Paul (opposite, introduced 1952) and Stratocaster (1954) that would become the staple tools of the genre, while the Fender Precision was the best-known bass. On its introduction in 1951, this began to replace the acoustic upright or 'doghouse' bass that had previously supplied rock'n'roll's bottom end.

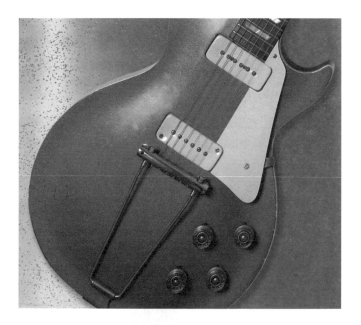

The Kinks came closest to creating metal when in 1964 they recorded 'You Really Got Me', a three-chord thrash whose aggressive tone was fortuitously created by slashing a loudspeaker cone in Dave Davies' guitar amp with a razorblade. His songwriter brother Ray had been inspired by seeing the Yardbirds at London's Marquee Club and that group, featuring (at various times) lead guitarists Eric Clapton,

Jeff Beck (below) and Jimmy Page, was one of the world's first hard-rock bands. Clapton's Les Paul guitar sound with his next group the Bluesbreakers was also highly influential on the generation of rock guitarists to come, while the Who introduced feedback effects to recordings like 'Anyway Anyhow Anywhere'.

The torch was picked up by Jimi Hendrix, the Jeff Beck Group and Cream. And while their music was still blues-based, the by-now massive amplification and spectacular stage shows – including destruction of guitars – created the cult of the 'guitar hero' and showed the way to a more outrageous future. In the States, the organ-heavy Vanilla Fudge and power trio Blue Cheer were approaching hard rock from a different direction, finding notoriety with versions of classic songs – the Supremes' 'You Keep Me Hanging On' (Fudge) and Eddie Cochran's 'Summertime Blues' (Blue Cheer) – that demonstrated the power of the new genre by turning them into hit singles.

But it was Jimi Hendrix, who would leave this earth all too prematurely in 1970, whose antics at Monterey and Woodstock were beamed to the world and inspired a generation to plug in and rock out. His music is still played and revered today.

The Seventies

The Seventies saw many different bands following in the footsteps of the departed Hendrix and now disbanded Cream. Led Zeppelin, Black Sabbath, Judas Priest and Deep Purple were among those to fill the vacuum; each produced one or two definitive albums that would be regarded as hard or heavy rock primers in the decades to come.

Sabbath, with their down-tuned guitars and satanic lyrics, were derided by the press but would prove far and away the most influential of these outfits in terms of inspiring musicians. Indeed, Sabbath's 'Paranoid' was one of the first examples of speed metal alongside Deep Purple's even more up-tempo 'Speed King'.

Queen and Aerosmith, now hard rock veterans, both released debut albums in 1973, the impressive playing of Brian May and Joe Perry elevating the guitarists to a status rivalling their showmen singers. Meanwhile, the Alice Cooper-inspired Kiss (below) showed they were more than just made-up pretty boys by, in 1975, pioneering the double live album format which would be used so successfully by Peter Frampton, Thin Lizzy and many other hard rockers.

Also in America, Lynyrd Skynyrd led the Southern Rock movement – Marshall Tucker, the Allman Brothers, Wet Willie and the Atlanta Rhythm Section among them – from below the Mason-Dixon line, sometimes incorporating up to three lead guitars into their line-up. The growth of guitar effects gave these bands an unrivalled palette of tones to use in making their music, but Eddie Van Halen inspired a move away from over-reliance on effects and studio trickery towards virtuosity when he developed the tapping technique. He picked up the baton laid down by Jeff Beck, who had similarly been the guitarist's guitarist of the early decade.

Motörhead peaked with live album 'No Sleep Till Hammersmith' that topped the UK chart on its release just into the Eighties. The use of a double bass drum pedal by Phil 'Philthy Animal' Taylor on tracks like 'Overkill' itself would prove influential on speed metal and associated genres.

The Eighties

A new wave of British heavy metal emerged in the early Eighties that would spawn the likes of Iron Maiden, Saxon and Def Leppard. Maiden led the field in introducing mythology and legend into their music, but this was taken even further by bands like Venom. Their *Black Metal* album spawned a genre by itself.

Germany was a major market for metal, home-grown heroes Accept leading the way. 'Fast As A Shark' on their 1982 album *Restless And Wild* showed the way to speed-metal hopefuls such as Running Wild, Grave Digger, Helloween, Rage and Paradox, while their countrymen, the Scorpions, continued in more traditional metal vein as they had through the Seventies.

Hard rock had an image that sold well in the shape of Bon Jovi who, unusually, sold as many singles as albums due to their female-friendly lyrics and image. Others like Skid Row and Poison followed in their wake while Ozzy Osbourne, by now long free of Black Sabbath, reinvented himself as a solo singer with help from virtuoso guitarist Randy Rhoads to add a new fan following to his traditional support. He had now edged towards hard rock from metal, but the music of his former band was inspiring a wave of mainly European outfits to explore doom and death metal.

Yngwie Malmsteen continued developing the virtuoso metal genre in the wake of Eddie Van Halen, while his native Scandinavia became an important rock hotbed in the late Eighties with the likes of Darkthrone and Mayhem from Norway pushing darker, more satanic messages. Meanwhile the newest sub-genre of progressive rock, prog metal, was developing via the likes of Queensrÿche,

Fates Warning and Watchtower. Labels like Magna Carta in the US and Inside Out in Europe would foster this combination of traditional musicianship and contemporary attack.

The Nineties

Guns N'Roses and Metallica were at opposite ends of the hard-rock spectrum, yet between them their success defined the early Nineties – indeed they even toured together. Both used radio and video to progress them from cult heroes to across-the-board rock giants, though this came more naturally to the charismatic Gunners than dark-clothed Metallica who held out against such sellout behaviour... until it made them superstars.

Grunge, with its punk-like 'universal access' that rejected instrumental virtuosity, enjoyed a brief work-shirted heyday – but while Kurt Cobain's death ensured Nirvana albums sold even more units, the genre did not sweep all aside as punk had 15 years earlier. Instead it brought some gifted musicians into the mainstream rock arena, not least Dave Grohl who traded drums for guitar and vocals with his next band, Foo Fighters.

The growth of alternative metal which had begun in the Eighties flowered with the success of such bands as Red Hot Chili Peppers, Rage Against the Machine, Living Colour, Primus and White Zombie. These all borrowed from black funk and fused its rhythms with metal guitar. Faith No More went further than most, their rock-rap-soul mix earning them three UK Top 10 albums. Grunge-era bands like Pearl Jam, Mother Love Bone, Temple of the Dog and Soundgarden also prospered thanks to a willingness to expand hard rock's cultural boundaries.

Black metal hit the headlines in Scandinavia with a series of deaths, murders and church-burnings, the rise of Norwegian bands such as Burzum, Satyricon, Immortal, Enslaved and Emperor being embroiled in this controversy. Speed and thrash metal lost some impetus as their proponents diversified into more specific genres or followed Metallica into the rock mainstream. Most bands still willing to serve under the heavy-metal banner were hardy survivors from previous decades like Uriah Heep or reformations like Deep Purple.

As the Nineties ended, American outfits like Limp Bizkit made a successful bid for the airwaves with their nu metal blend of rock and rap. Korn and Papa Roach followed their lead, and the whole movement peaked in 2000 with Bizkit's *Chocolate Starfish And The Hot Dog Flavored Water* and Roach's triple-platinum *Infest*.

The Noughties

In nu rock's last defiant roar, Linkin Park's *Hybrid Theory* was the best-selling album of 2001 with sales of more than five million, but the genre suffered commercial meltdown thereafter. Radio stations that had put the genre on the map turned against it as a host of similar-sounding bands like American Head Charge, Primer 55, Adema, Cold, the Union Underground, Dope, Apartment 26, Hed (Planet Earth) and Skrape had swamped the airwaves. What was innovative and sounded different two years previously was suddenly everywhere, not helped by the major labels jumping on the bandwagon. But as rock is by nature cyclical, it may well come again.

Reinvented bands were a safer short-term bet, and they ruled the charts in the new millennium. Leading lights were Audioslave, which consisted of Rage Against the Machine instrumentalists fronted

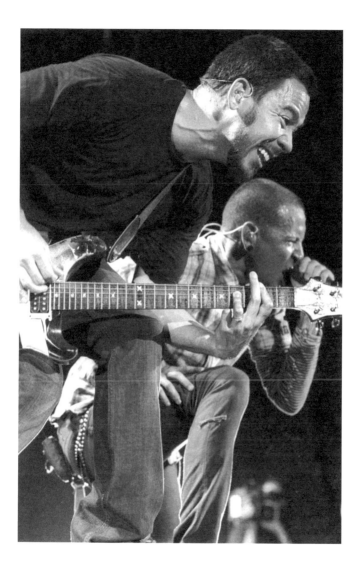

by former Soundgarden singer Chris Cornell and Velvet Revolver, made up of ex-members of Stone Temple Pilots and Guns N'Roses. No-frills hard rock made a comeback in the shape of Canadians Nickelback, whose 'How You Remind Me' was one of Y2K's rock anthems.

Downloading was fast becoming the standard means of acquiring music, which presented rock's heavier genres with the challenge of appealing to a new, techno-savvy generation. Among those who met it were Scots, Biffy Clyro, whose melodic hard rock ticked many boxes and whose success justified their switching to a major label in 2006. They played support dates to Muse, another very smart 'noughties' band whose wide appeal compensated for their inability to be pigeonholed. Their MySpace page labels them 'alternative progressive rock', which covers several bases. Their fame rests on their live show, which is surely credible enough.

The Red Hot Chili Peppers were still the highest-profile alternative metal act and they had earned their stadium-filling status. But in many ways hard rock was looking back to move forward. The Darkness sustained a brief success by enrolling Queen's producer and winding the clock back to 'Bohemian Rhapsody' – but the fact that Led Zeppelin's re-formation for a 40th anniversary concert in London in late 2007 was the hottest ticket of the year suggested there was nothing like the real thing.

And rock, whichever way you slice it, is *still* the real deal...

Further Reading

Chappell, J., *Rock Guitar For Dummies*, John Wiley & Sons, 2001; Heatley, M. (Gen. Ed.), *The Definitive Encyclopedia of Rock*, Flame Tree Publishing, 2006; Jake Jackson (Ed.)., *Guitar Chords*, Flame Tree Publishing, 2006; Heatley, M., *How to Write Great Songs*, Flame Tree Publishing, 2007; Johnston, R., *How to Play Rock Guitar: The Basics and Beyond*, Backbeat Books, 2003; Johnston, R., *How to Play Metal Guitar: The Basics and Beyond*, Backbeat Books, 2004; Kitts, J., & Tolinski, B., *Nu-Metal (Guitar World Presents)*, Hal Leonard Publishing Corporation, 2002; Leonard, M., *The Illustrated Complete Guitar Handbook*, Flame Tree Publishing, 2007; Mulford, P., *Fast Forward Metal Bass Styles*, Wise Publications, 1997; Stetina, T., *Metal Rhythm Guitar Vol. 1*, Hal Leonard Publishing Corporation, 1992; Stetina, T., *Metal Lead Guitar Vol. 1*, Hal Leonard Publishing Corporation, 1995; Stetina, T., *Total Rock Guitar: A Complete Guide to Learning Rock Guitar*, Hal Leonard Publishing Corporation, 2001; Wolfsohn, M. P., *The Ultimate Rock Guitar Scale Finder*, Hal Leonard Corporation, 2007.

Internet Sites

www.chordie.com Large collection of guitar chords and tabs; *www.guitarconsultant.com*. Online free guitar lessons and home study courses; *www.guitarmetal.com*. Metal style guitar lessons and discussion; *www.themetalforge.com* Heavy metal and hard rock magazine with news, interviews and reviews; *www.metalunderground.com* News, reviews and interviews from the industry and bands; *www.rockmagic.net*. Tablature for all the main bands plus lyrics and a store.